show me a
STORY

show me a STORY

40 Craft Projects
and Activities
to Spark Children's
Storytelling

EMILY K. NEUBURGER

Storey Publishing

The mission of Storey Publishing is to serve our customers by publishing practical information that encourages personal independence in harmony with the environment.

Edited by **Deborah Balmuth and Pam Thompson**
Art direction and book design by **Carolyn Eckert**
Text production by **Jennifer Jepson Smith**

Cover photography by © **Buff Strickland:** front (bottom three), back (author), inside front (row 1: right), and inside back (row 1: left, center left, right; row 2: left, center left, center right; row 3: center right, right; and row 4: center left); **Greg Nesbit Photography:** spine, inside front (row 1: center left, center right; row 2: left, center left, center right; row 3: center right, right; and row 4: all), and inside back (row 1: center right; row 2: right; row 3: left, center left, and row 4: left, center right, right); **John Polak Photography:** inside front (row 1: left; row 2: right; and row 3: left, center left); and © **Tara Gorman:** front (top) and back (top)

Interior photography credits appear on page 140

Crafting and photo styling of cover, backcover, chapter openers and gate folds by **Tara Gorman**

All projects and illustrations by the author, except for those on page 138, middle and bottom, by **Martin Gentes**

Indexed by **Nancy D. Wood**

The information in this book is true and complete to the best of our knowledge. All recommendations are made without guarantee on the part of the author or Storey Publishing. The author and publisher disclaim any liability in connection with the use of this information.

Storey books are available for special premium and promotional uses and for customized editions. For further information, please call 1-800-793-9396.

Storey Publishing
210 MASS MoCA Way
North Adams, MA 01247
www.storey.com

Printed in China by R.R. Donnelley
10 9 8 7 6 5 4 3 2 1

Library of Congress Cataloging-in-Publication Data
Neuburger, Emily K.
  Show me a story / by Emily K. Neuburger.
    p. cm.
  Includes bibliographical references and index.
  ISBN 978-1-60342-988-7 (pbk. : alk. paper)
  ISBN 978-1-61212-148-2 (hardcover : alk. paper)
  1. Handicraft for children—Juvenile literature. 2. Storytelling—Juvenile literature. I. Title.
TT160.N456 2012
745.5083—dc23
                              2012004610

In memory of Nanny Ruth, my favorite storyteller.
I remember. I will always remember.

And for Leah Rose and Hazel Ruth. You are what my heart dreamed of many moons ago.
And you are what my heart will dream of many moons from now.

contents

preface / 8

introduction / 11
Tell More Stories
    (They're Good for You) / 12
Be Inspired / 14
Play! / 15
Go! / 16
Observe! / 17
Using This Book / 18

1 story starters / 21
Story Disks / 23
Cut and Tell / 29
Story Pool / 30
Story Dice / 32
Story Blocks / 34
The Parts of a Story / 36
Beginning, Middle, End / 38
Story Grab Bag / 40
These Are the Stories in
    My Neighborhood / 43
Magnetic Story Board / 48
Story Sparks / 50

2 story evolution / 55
Story Stones / 57
Traveling Puppet Theater / 60
Memory Cards / 63
Story Mat / 66
Storytelling Jar / 69
Storybook / 72
Story City / 77
Story Map / 80
Story Soundtrack / 82
Storytelling Kit / 83

3 story activities / 85
Storytelling Walk / 87
Picture Tales / 89
Truth or Tale? / 90
Fill In the Blanks / 92
Story-Disk Chain / 94
Build a Story / 96
Word Tags / 98
Word Lists / 100
The Reference Desk / 103
Create the Past / 104
Story Ping-Pong / 106
1, 2, 3 Scribble & Tell / 107
Story Timeline / 108
Timing Is Everything / 110

4 story play / 113
Magical Mailbox / 115
Magic Pebbles / 117
Magic Flower Wand / 118
Story Sets / 120
Adventure Kit / 123
Story Scenery / 126

materials / 129
templates / 132
puppet theater / 136
puppets / 137
photo credits / 140
acknowledgments / 141
index / 142
puppet theater backgrounds / 145

preface

When I was a child, the stories inside my head were what drove my play — they were the scripts of my childhood. I grew up in the urban suburbs where I was hard pressed to find true woodlands. That didn't matter to me, though. I would disappear into the narrow strip of trees and grass that was our side yard and convince myself that I was on a long, windy wagon ride across the prairie. I would set up camp in the barely there grass next to a row of divider hedges and some old rakes. Without much room to play in, I claimed this tightly enclosed space as my own.

Once my campfire of twigs and leaves was set up, I would use a jagged-edged rock to crack open smooth stones, my freshly farmed potatoes. The halved potatoes would slowly roast on the pretend fire as I stirred my big pot of water, weed, and dirt soup. I was fully immersed in my imaginary world, lost in my own tale of survival and solitude, making the most of my natural surroundings. Reality was suspended, and I happily slipped into telling my own story — again and again until I felt like I had memorized my place, and I was ready to find myself somewhere else in time and space. I want my children to have that. I want them to make up their own games, to find inspiration from what's around them, to create their own imaginary worlds.

ABOVE: Me, with my daughters, Hazel and Leah, telling a story together.

As I grew older, I found it harder to access those imaginary worlds that were so easy to find when I was ten. I became busy with deadlines, school, working late, meetings, and picnicking with friends. It wasn't until the end of college, when I took two writing classes with one of the university's resident poets, that I reconnected with the familiar feeling of being lost in my own imaginary world. She nudged us on with unique and creative writing exercises and encouraged us to become inspired. I sketched with my left hand. I gave strangers my handmade gifts. I wrote one poem a day. I woke in the morning and recorded my dreams in a journal and fervently used that material to write poems and stories in the afternoon. It was an inspiring time that showed me that being an adult doesn't mean that you have to stop spending time with your imagination. Go burrowing in search, and you will find it.

And so it was true, years later, when my first sweet-cheeked daughter entered the world. Except this time, I didn't need to burrow very far. Just watching her big, hazel eyes widen and sparkle as she gazed at picture books with talking hedgehogs and ducks was enough for me. I was instantly inspired, and it resonated deep, deep within. This little person was so curious and captivated, and she was ready. She wanted to meet new characters, be invited into fairy woodlands, and hear about the most wild, raucous adventures. Witnessing her creative spark — the way she intuitively craved new stories and how she begged for her favorites again and again — marked a turning point for me.

As both of my daughters grow older and I listen to their chatter about queens, dragons, and imaginary villages, my path to crafting and story-telling is illuminated. I fill rooms with art materials and story sparks, and I teach my students to listen to their own creative voices. I watch as they imagine deeply, create fully, and gain confidence, and I feel centered. They tell me stories about a black sea with waves that lull, towers that stretch to the moon, and complicated underground rabbit villages. It's true — listening to a child's earnest storytelling makes me happy.

—EMILY K. NEUBURGER

once upon a time, there was a magical land . . .

introduction

Children have bits of stories floating around inside their heads: tales of dropped ice-cream cones and flocks of birds plotting their route across the sky, time-traveling cars, and chipmunks setting up tidy homes inside tunnels. They might be simple stories that stem from the day or more complex fantasies born of hours of contemplation. Whether their ideas are jotted down in a journal or just float across their minds — really, all that matters is that these little nuggets of curiosity and interest exist. These pieces of narrative, the stories on the *inside*, can be explored, and with just a bit of planning and lots of joyful intention, they can become the stories on the *outside*.

Storytelling is the perfect, most nourishing food for growing minds. When you think about what you remember of the concepts and lessons you've learned in life, the ones that come to mind tend to be attached to stories. This is because they engaged your mind and helped you make sense of the world. The activities and projects in this book are not just for children; they are also meant to inspire and encourage the adults who love, teach, and care for them. With these projects and this approach, adults and children can be happily hooked into a world of storytelling.

Trust your imagination. Walk openly into the unknown land of a story.

Tell More Stories (They're Good for You)

Old-Time Tales

When you are stumped for an imaginative tale for your children, tell a story about your own past. Personal stories are often their favorite ones to hear. These stories tell of mistakes, triumphs, lessons learned, sorrows, and joys, and it thrills children to imagine seemingly all-powerful adults as the smaller creatures we once were.

Exercise Creativity

When children tell stories, their inventive minds explore unique ways to frame and develop ideas. Trees can long for their newly fallen leaves. A bee family can prepare dinner after a long day in the hive. When children first recognize their freedom to create, it changes the energy in the room. In one of my storytelling workshops, a small group of children realized one day that a character could be a *thing*. At first the room was silent. Then the chatter steadily increased until the children were bubbling with yelps and ideas. "A storm! *That* can be a character!" one of the children exclaimed. The magic of creativity exists in the moment that someone realizes that she can imagine beyond her own expectations.

Expand Emotional Awareness

Stories serve as powerful tools for children as they work to understand and interact with the world around them. Children test their own feelings by creating characters who act in their stead. When they listen to the stories of others, they have a chance to experience and label their feelings in new and clarifying ways. One child's story might describe a character as "mellow" or "tense," giving her friend who's never before heard of these personality traits a new language for her own feelings. You might notice that after a child experiences an intense emotion — loss, grief, anger, or jealousy — some of that powerful feeling will be woven into her storytelling.

Practice Communicating

Storytelling helps children develop important language, communication, and listening skills. Children may start out simply sharing bits of stories — characters, names, and moments. As they grow, they begin to link these pieces to create more-detailed stories with beginnings and ends. This facilitates natural, creative dialogue in daily conversations.

Using pictures and words to tell stories prepares children for written composition as well. They practice using new and familiar vocabulary and grammatical structures. They also learn about metaphorical language — that something might stand in for something else. Magic stones and sharp-toothed monsters appear in stories not only as themselves but also as symbols or metaphors for things such as truth and greed.

Make Connections

When children share their stories, imaginary or real, they are offering up their own questions, concerns, joys, worries, and hopes. They watch as others respond to their stories, and this empowers them to become more invested in their own creative process.

Telling stories encourages family members to laugh together and relate to each other. Not surprisingly, some of

Face Your Fears

Many of the spooky creatures that frighten my daughters at night make their way into their stories in the safe daylight. Almost always, the pesky creatures are captured and taught an important lesson. After the dust settles, my girls witness their own resilience and strength.

our most meaningful and treasured stories are those that are passed down in our families. They help us have a sense of our heritage and culture. Small, salient details — a creamy blue tablecloth, a fistful of checkers, the cracking sound of a breaking chair leg — live on in the stories that are passed down from generation to generation. They are what helps us remember!

Solve Problems

When children find ways for their characters to resolve sticky situations, they learn that one problem can have many solutions. A lonely, forlorn duck can perk herself up by hosting a duck party or by swimming in the duck Olympics or by saying hello to every duck she encounters that day. There are so many options. Phew!

Develop Moral Thinking

Stories give children the opportunity to think about morals, lessons, and conflict resolution. With practice, children begin to search for the moral at the end of a story, and some will even structure their own stories around a specific message. Children who listen and tell many stories begin to recognize trends in human behavior. Their perspectives expand, and they become more critical, observant thinkers. They begin to consider, in broader terms, what it means to be helpful, mean, practical, hopeful, spiteful, or considerate. Creating characters — which teaches that multiple perspectives really do exist *at every moment* — gives children invaluable tools for understanding others and for finding their way in the world.

Be Inspired

I am most inspired when I give myself the time to observe and contemplate the world around me, and this is true for children too.

In order to make room for inspiring thoughts and ideas, it is usually best to keep things simple. Isn't it funny that you can purchase a seemingly perfect educational toy, but an ordinary trinket ends up being the gateway to hours of imaginative play? Often the most common, everyday situation or object elicits the most complex story. Acorns, for example, can be little people, a food supply for weary travelers, medicine for the sick, decorations for a party, or simply acorns in a forest of hungry animals waiting for their dinner. The space between a wingback chair and a side table can be a compact, cozy space shuttle, a rabbit's burrow, or the driver's seat in a racecar.

Inspiration can come when you aren't trying, within silences and empty spaces. Model this for children. Teach them to trust the pauses, themselves, and their own creative process. Show them that when you have patience and confidence, inspiration will come. Encourage journal jotting, note taking, chatting, sketching and doodling, and impromptu story-game playing to open their minds to new imaginative worlds.

What about the times when you're trying *very hard*? When you feel as if you've nudged your mind as far as it will go, when you're convinced that the empty space forever will be a gaping hole of nothingness — then, too, inspiration can wiggle its way in. Teach children not to give up when something feels really hard. Model this, too. Encourage them to get past their hurdles. Give the character a name, figure out where the mouse family lives, explain why the sad lion is suddenly happy, and decide the name of the town before putting aside a story. If they stop at the tricky parts, they risk missing out on the clever ideas that tend to pop up during those moments of brain tension.

HAVE CONFIDENCE!

Do you feel critical of the stories you end up telling? When you tell an impromptu story to your children, does your brain mutter curmudgeonly bits like, "I can't believe I'm telling another one about fairies casting a spell in the woods. Snore." or "Sam the puppy again?" If that happens, give yourself a break and do away with the pressure and judgments. That kind of thinking prohibits you from being free to imagine widely, and the less you judge or pressure yourself, the more available you'll be for a deeper creative journey.

Play!

Engaging in open-ended creative play is a great way to spark imaginative thinking. Consider a child gathering a bouquet of flowers in the backyard. As he picks dandelions, wild daisies, and violets, he is close to the ground, looking at the grass, bugs, and pinecones. Seeing his surroundings from a different perspective is bound to get him thinking creatively about the world around him.

- Float sticks and leaves in a stream or puddle.
- Make a crown of branches and twigs.
- Play with a map.
- Listen to old records.
- Make important signs for imaginary things.
- Go on a walk in search of five interesting things.
- Set a fancy table and eat a royal meal.
- Make a terrarium.

- Play in a tidal pool at the ocean.
- Put clothes on a pet (if she doesn't mind).
- Look at dinosaur bones at a museum.
- Keep a dream journal with drawings and words.
- Flip through an old set of encyclopedias.
- Turn a big cardboard box into a boat.
- Spread blankets on the floor and make a pretend ocean.

Go!

Ask children to make a "Places That Inspire Me" list, and visit the ones that are realistically possible. (Going to the moon might have to wait until a later date.)

Here's mine:

- ➤ the forest
- ➤ tag sales
- ➤ museums
- ➤ a paper recycling bin
- ➤ small towns
- ➤ thrift stores
- ➤ the ocean
- ➤ a national park
- ➤ where people constantly come and go (train station, airport, and bus stop)
- ➤ art and stationery shops
- ➤ fabric stores
- ➤ historical villages
- ➤ a stream
- ➤ new (to me) towns, cities, and countries
- ➤ trains

Observe!

While you're on one of these field trips, encourage the children to look at their surroundings with full concentration. Challenge them to observe for at least five minutes, and once everyone feels saturated by the surroundings, suggest that the children sketch or write about their discoveries in their journals. Their sketches can be literal or abstract; all that matters is that the essence of the inspiration is recorded. Sometimes I sketch an object or a scene, and because I have only a pencil or pen, I'll write the names of the colors with little arrows pointing to specific parts of my drawing. The idea is for the children to record what feels most interesting so they can remember and use it later in their creations.

CARRY A JOURNAL . . . AND A CAMERA

Stash a small journal and pencil in your bag for spontaneous moments of observation. Don't take the risk of forgetting them by the time you return home!

Using a camera to capture your surroundings can be the perfect way to reflect on the inspiring places and objects that were unable to make the trip back to your home or school. It is also a nice way to search for inspiration after the fact. There are times when I feel overwhelmed by all of the beauty around me, which causes me to have a difficult time deciphering what is most intriguing or loveliest. A digital camera makes it easy for me to take lots of pictures of the journey so that later I can spend quiet time remembering and reflecting on what I saw. If you have an extra camera lying around, consider lending it to a child for her adventures. This is also a nice way for adults to see the world through children's eyes. You can ask them questions about why they took certain pictures and to tell you what kinds of ideas they bring to mind.

Using This Book

The 40 projects and activities in *Show Me a Story* are designed to help children begin, develop, and play with storytelling. I wrote the book for anyone who spends time with children — parents, teachers, aunts and uncles, grandparents, camp counselors, spiritual leaders, therapists, childcare workers, psychologists, babysitters. Though I give plenty of modifications and suggestions for children ages three to five, most of the activities are designed for children ages five through early adolescence.

For each project and activity, I suggest the youngest age that it seems likely children will be able to engage purposefully. Of course, younger children are always encouraged to dabble and participate in whatever way they choose. All projects and activities are intended for children with varying degrees of parent and teacher participation. For craft projects, I suggest an age for the making and another age for the playing, when they differ.

Have Fun with the Projects

As parents and teachers, our role is to follow children's natural inclinations and enthusiasm. As you engage and involve children in these activities, pay attention to what excites them and do your best to tailor the projects to their interests. Finding out what materials inspire and engage a child, and using those specific materials to create a new storytelling toy, can be magical. Not only will the child love the new toy, but she will also love what it is made out of. She will be enticed by the feel of the stone, or she will fondly remember getting to tear up a magazine into teeny pieces until her fingers felt numb. If a child is particularly interested in outer space, you could encourage him to make a Storytelling Jar (page 69) with white and tan felt for the moon and craters and a rocket ship dangling from overhead. If a child is interested in sports, you might encourage her to make a Story Mat (page 66) that has an Olympic park with a ski jump, an ice rink, a toboggan run, and snowboarding ramps. And, of course, she'd have to whip up some Olympiad Story Stone people (page 57) to take part in all of the events.

As children build stories, don't fuss about grammar and spelling too much; doing so might inhibit the creative process. If teachers and home-schooling parents want to make comments about grammar and spelling, wait until after the story is told. As children's storytelling gains momentum, it can be discouraging and frustrating for them to have to pause to figure out the spelling of a word. Even worse, they might forget where their story was heading.

And don't fret if a child seems stuck or particularly challenged by a story line. The truth is, feeling frustrated or unsatisfied can lead to deeper thinking. Often storytelling gets interesting just when a child feels like giving up, so encourage her to keep trying.

All Good Stories Take Time

With all the story projects, I give an estimate of the time they'll take to make. But using the projects is not a time-specified activity. Creativity doesn't run on a clock! Let the children guide you. When I specify "hands-on" time, that's because you may need more time to let parts dry while you do something else; in these cases, the start-to-finish time is longer.

You'll find that many of the projects in this book can be made with materials you have on hand in your pantry, cabinets, backyard, drawers, and recycling bin. In my creations, I use as many repurposed and found objects as possible. Consult Materials (page 129) for more information about craft supplies before you get started.

The beauty of these projects and activities lies in their simplicity and creativity. I hope that instructions and vivid pictures will draw you into the possibility of making and doing them for your own storytelling. As you read, plan, and become inspired, remember that this book is meant to be a collaborative experience for children and adults. Share your thoughts and ideas with the young storytellers, and invite them to share their ideas. Show them the projects and have them read the instructions. The more involved they are in the process, the more invested and engaged they will be.

. . . with whom would the mouse share this perfect piece of cheese?

1 story starters

creative prompts
to help children
begin telling stories

Stories are the creative conversion of life itself into a more powerful, clearer, more meaningful experience. — ROBERT MCKEE

The beginning of a story isn't always easy to find. Sometimes we circle and circle, searching for a way in, and if the entrance eludes us, we move on. This is true for both adults and children, so I started thinking: What if it were easier to begin? These Story Starters are born from this vision; they are meant to turn children into empowered storytellers who, even in the midst of drawing a blank, can conjure up something new and enjoy the process.

Play with these crafts and games, and they will offer ways to generate fresh stories. Of course, age determines how involved children can be. Children ages five and up can make an entire set of Story Disks (page 23) with adult guidance, whereas younger children might help to generate lists of characters and objects and do part of the painting. Any amount of participation will have children feeling engaged and motivated. When they make these projects, I think you'll notice that they will take on more ownership of their stories.

→ *There isn't one right way.*

How to Use

Please use the Story Starters in any way that feels inspiring and purposeful. Teachers, use them as creative writing prompts or as engaging ways to access nouns and verbs. Parents and children, use them to begin a story at birthday parties, at play dates, or during quiet story times. Our family likes to use the Story Dice (page 32) to tell stories after dinner. We toss the dice and let the unique combinations direct our verbal adventure. Some of our stories are full of adventure and plot, others end up silly or farcical. Not only is this okay — I encourage it! It teaches children that there isn't one right way to tell a story. And please, as your story time winds down, don't feel as if you have to package your story with a nice, tidy ending. It really is about the creative process, the funny moment, the silly character, the sly solution. Focus on being present and true.

Story Disks

These wooden disks, decorated with pictures of nifty characters, things, and places, are compact idea generators. They serve as perfect little sources of inspiration. Make as many as you want, pass some on to your neighbor, trade them with friends, tuck them in pockets, or give them as gifts. They make people smile.

TIME
To make:
2 hands-on hours

AGES
To make: **5+**

To use: **3+**

PLAYERS
1+

HOW TO MAKE

1. Paint both sides of each wooden disk with a cheery color. (I like to make several groups of six, with each set the same color.) Hold a disk between two fingers as you paint it with the other hand.

MATERIALS

- acrylic paint and brushes
- 1½" wooden disks (see Materials, page 129)
- plastic containers (from the recycling bin)
- paper scraps
- pencil
- scissors
- mini-muffin tin (for organizing collage materials)
- Mod Podge
- foam brush
- toothpick
- wax paper
- thin black marker
- eraser
- small stamps
- black ink pad

2. To dry them with the least amount of smudging, set up a few plastic containers from your recycling bin (think hummus or cream-cheese tubs) and stand the disks in them on end, leaning against the sides. For a nice solid finish, let them dry overnight and then apply a second coat of paint in the morning. Or if you aren't worried about imperfection, one coat is just fine.

While you are waiting for the disks to dry, write down a list of interesting, imaginative characters, places, and things. Later, if you find yourself searching for ideas, you'll have this list to help direct your creative process.

3. Once the disks are dry, add tiny pictures, using any of these three techniques: collage, drawing and painting, or stamping. Mix and match, or stick with the style that feels most satisfying to you. Don't get hemmed in — try them all and see which ones work best for your storytelling.

Collaged Pictures

1. Decide how to break up your collaged image. For example, if your image is a tree, you might cut the trunk out of one color paper, the leaves out of another, and the fruit or flowers out of a third.

2. Draw the image pieces on the back of each piece of paper with the pencil, then carefully cut out each piece. To keep all of the pieces of an image together, a mini-muffin tin or small paper cup works nicely.

3. With the foam brush, apply one coat of Mod Podge to your disk, place the first paper piece down, and brush another layer of Mod Podge over it. Continue layering Mod Podge and paper pieces until all are applied. If it's difficult to pick up those tiny bits of paper, nudge them into place with a toothpick. Place the disk on wax paper to dry overnight.

▶ TEACHING TIP

Story Disks are an engaging way to teach vocabulary. Once you have the images on your disks, print the corresponding words on the other side. (Use pencil first!)

Drawn and Painted Pictures

1. With a pencil, lightly sketch your design onto the disk. Once you're pleased with the image, fill it in with paint. Place the disk on wax paper and let dry for at least three hours.

2. Once the disks are completely dry, outline the image with a thin black marker to give it more definition. If your hand wobbles while drawing, don't fret: this gives your images personality!

3. Very gently erase extra pencil lines, being mindful not to smudge the marker and paint.

Stamped Pictures

1. Choose a selection of small stamps (less than 1½" wide) for the disks.

2. Dip a stamp into the ink and use the tips of your fingers to press it firmly and evenly onto a disk. It's a good idea to do a few practice stamps before attempting the real deal. If you find you're missing the *perfect* stamp to complete your Story Disk set, use a thin black marker to draw an image. It will fit right in with the stamped aesthetic.

MOD PODGE TIPS

➤ Apply in thin layers.

➤ In order to avoid wrinkling, apply Mod Podge to the back of the cut-out paper, press firmly, and smooth out bubbles. Wait 15 to 20 minutes and then apply a top coat of Mod Podge. This will give the paper time to set before you saturate it with the top coat.

➤ When you first apply Mod Podge, it will be milky white and opaque. Don't fret! It will dry perfectly clear, like magic.

➤ Allow the Mod Podge to dry fully before playing with or using the project.

HOW TO USE

There are so many engaging, creative ways to use these disks. Here are a few ideas:

1. Lay several facedown on a table, then flip them over, one at a time, to reveal the next piece of an ongoing story.

2. Put the disks in a bag and have a child pick out three of them to be used in a bigger story.

3. Lay the disks faceup on the table as visual inspiration for starting and continuing a story.

other neat ideas

>> Give a set of Story Disks and a small journal as a gift.

>> Experiment with other collage materials, such as fabric, seeds, and bits of fiber.

>> Make a Story Disk necklace. This is a favorite among my friends and loved ones (including my daughters). Using a drill with a very small bit, make a hole at the top of a disk. Put some necklace cording through the hole, then put a clasp on the ends or tie a simple knot.

Cut and Tell

This simple activity is quick and fun to prepare, and children love that there are surprises on the other side of the squares. Children cut random squares out of various printed papers, then use them to tell stories. Because this project calls for materials often already on hand, it's a great rainy- or sick-day activity.

TIME
To make: 1 hour

AGES
To make: 4+

To use: 3+

PLAYERS
2+

MATERIALS
- pages from old magazines (nature, craft, lifestyle, food, adventure, travel, catalogs)
- pages from dilapidated illustrated books to cut up
- ruler
- pencil
- scissors

HOW TO MAKE

1. Lay out all your magazine pages so that the sides with the most interesting images are facing down. (That's right: You can't see them.)

2. On the back side, use the ruler and pencil to randomly mark 5" squares.

3. Cut along the pencil lines, trying not to peek at the interesting images, then stack up the squares.

Younger children can cut without measuring and shouldn't be concerned with making exact squares. Because they are randomly cutting, some squares may end up with no image or half of an image, so be prepared to toss those into the recycling bin. Still, don't look: The imperfection of the activity is part of what makes it exciting.

HOW TO USE

1. Each storyteller is given 10 to 12 squares, with the interesting images facedown.

2. One storyteller begins by flipping over an image and beginning a story. As the story continues, the storyteller flips over another image and continues narrating, doing his best to incorporate each image into the story.

3. Once the first storyteller has finished, the next storyteller constructs his story, based on his images.

other neat ideas

>> Do Cut and Tell as a group activity, taking turns flipping over an image and continuing the story, each child picking up where the previous child left off.

>> Organize pictures by theme, color, or design and use these new groups to tell stories.

>> Encourage children to cut and trade squares with each other for an open-ended, collaborative storytelling experience.

Story Pool

This activity is designed to be played by a group of children, who will work together to build the key components of a story.

TIME
To make: **2 hours**

AGES
To make: **5+**

To use: **5+**

PLAYERS
3+

MATERIALS
- pencil
- cardboard, approximately 18" × 36"
- craft knife
- blue paint and brushes
- scissors
- several sheets of colored paper (different colors)
- art marker
- double-sided tape

HOW TO MAKE

1. To make the Story Pool, with a pencil draw the shape of a wavy, irregular body of water on the large piece of cardboard and use a craft knife to cut it out. (With adult supervision!)

2. Paint the cardboard with blue paint.

3. While the paint is drying, make the Story Tickets. Cut small squares (approximately 3") from the colored paper (enough for each child to have five squares).

4. Ask each child to draw or collage a story element on each ticket (animals, people, places, things, feelings, for example). See Story Sparks (page 50) if you need ideas. Be sure that every image is labeled, by either the children or an adult.

HOW TO USE

1. Children sit in front of the pool, with five tickets each.

2. The first child places a piece of double-sided tape onto the back of a ticket and puts it in the Story Pool. As each child adds an element to the pool, the group develops the contents of a story.

3. Story Tickets are added to the pool until the group feels they make a well-balanced beginning of a story. Not all tickets have to be added. Children should judiciously add tickets to the pool.

other **neat** ideas

» The group of children can write a collaborative story based on their Story Pool.

» A parent or teacher can add one or two surprise elements to the pool.

» Focus the storytelling by providing a specific theme or topic for the Story Tickets.

Story Dice

Throw the dice and let chance play a role in your storytelling. Use these dice alone or with a group to develop a story.

TIME
To make: **1 hour**

AGES
To make: **5+**

To use: **3+**

PLAYERS
1+

HOW TO MAKE

Make a list of possible characters, things, and places you would like on the dice. Narrow down the list and select the exact images you want printed. You can make each die display only one category: characters, places, things, magical items, weather descriptions, for example. Or you can make varied dice that have characters, things, and places on a single die. The benefit of making category

Stamped Die

Illustrated Dice

MATERIALS

- ➤ paper and pencils
- ➤ tiny stamps
- ➤ black ink
- ➤ small (approximately ¾") wooden cubes (see Materials, page 129)
- ➤ fine-tip ballpoint pen
- ➤ colored pencils

POSSIBLE CATEGORIES AND IMAGES

- ➤ characters (person, monster, fish, bee)
- ➤ things (telephone, candle, book, bucket)
- ➤ weather descriptions (clouds, raindrops, snowflake, wind)
- ➤ places (ocean, woods, house, school)
- ➤ numbers (100, 3, 10, 2)
- ➤ food (cupcake, Swiss cheese, pizza, eggs)
- ➤ feelings (depicted with a mouth or face)
- ➤ tools (wrench, hammer, rope, ruler)
- ➤ animals (moth, rabbit, mole, lion)
- ➤ magical items (pebbles, wand, dust, web)
- ➤ clothing (tee shirt, boots, overalls, gloves)
- ➤ natural objects (tree, bird's nest, mushroom, mountain)

dice, though, is that you can roll two and know for sure that you'll get one character and one thing. If you roll varied dice, you could end up with two places or two weather descriptions.

Stamped Dice

Dip the stamp into the ink, and use the tips of your fingers to press it firmly and evenly onto each die.

Illustrated Dice

Draw the outline of each image with a fine-tip ballpoint pen. (Avoid using art markers because they tend to bleed a bit too much.) Fill in with colored pencils.

HOW TO USE

1. If you are playing by yourself, simply roll the dice and use the combination to begin your story. When you find yourself running out of ideas, roll the dice again for a new combination. If you are playing as a group, take turns rolling the dice and incorporating your combination into the larger story.

2. Keep in mind that six dice can present 36 different images and 46,656 unique combinations. Yowza! The more dice you add to your collection, the more possible combinations, which, in turn, lead to seemingly endless storytelling options.

other neat ideas

➤➤ Break out the Story Dice when you're entertaining, and use them as an after-dinner game.

➤➤ Package them in pairs with a small notebook, and give them as a party favor or as a gift.

➤➤ Bring along a few pairs in the car for long road trips. Take turns rolling them on top of a book, and use the various combinations to tell stories.

TEACHING TIP   Have all of the students in your class make a set for their creative writing assignments. To add a bit of fun and variety, have students trade their Story Dice or one Story Die with their neighbors. You just might start a school trend!

Story Blocks

Turn plain wooden blocks into movable storytelling prompts.
Line up the blocks in a certain order and use them to tell a story.
Take turns, and the next person can rearrange the blocks and
tell a different story. It's a natural way to develop a story — just
line 'em up and begin.

TIME
To make: **2 hands-on hours**

AGES
To make: **5+**

To use: **3+**

PLAYERS
1+

There is something very satisfying about
the heft of these blocks. When your children add new characters to their stories,
they feel the weight of the characters
in their hands as they place them in the
storytelling lineup. These blocks give
children a chance to use their bodies
and their brains. Educators and therapists who work with young children will
appreciate this balanced combination
of gross-motor and cognitive skills.

TEACHING TIP During creative writing lessons, teachers can put the
blocks on display and encourage students to choose some for their writing tables.

HOW TO MAKE

MATERIALS

- wooden blocks, used or new
- sandpaper
- acrylic paint and brushes
- stain (optional)
- pictures from catalogs, magazines, maps, personal drawings
- colored pencils or pens (optional)
- pencil
- scissors
- Mod Podge
- foam brush

1. Depending on the finish on the blocks, you may need to rough them up with a bit of sandpaper. Select pleasing, inviting colors for the blocks. You can paint them in a variety of colors, all the same color, or different shades of one color, as you wish. Paint three sides of the blocks, and stand them up on the unpainted side to dry.

2. Once they're dry, paint the unpainted side and set aside to dry. Repeat this process until all the blocks are well coated in paint. Do you want to leave the blocks in their natural state? Go for it! Or use a stain rather than opaque paint, so that the wood grain shows through. The more the blocks are tailored to your individual taste, the better.

3. Sort through images and choose ones that seem interesting, creative, funny, or just darn cute. You can use drawn images as well.

4. Given that the blocks are most likely of different sizes and shapes, take care to match each one individually with a picture. Choose a block and then look through the magazines for an image that would fit on it nicely. Use the pencil and a block to lightly trace an outline around the image, but cut out the image a bit smaller than the outline. Don't fret about imperfection while you cut: a little bit of uneven cutting will add character and life to your Story Blocks.

5. With a foam brush, coat the front of a block with a thin layer of Mod Podge and firmly press the picture onto it. Carefully press out any air bubbles and wrinkles, then coat with another layer of Mod Podge. Set on a cloth to dry. Once the blocks are dry, you may need to give them all another coat of Mod Podge to ensure their longevity.

other neat ideas

>> Set a few Story Blocks on a windowsill, dresser, or shelf for a bit of story art, and change them from time to time to keep things interesting.

>> With little ones, encourage creative building, rearranging, and stacking.

>> Add a few Story Blocks with words to your child's collection. This will add depth to the storytelling possibilities.

THE PARTS OF A STORY

SETTING

Setting includes not only place but time, situation, and atmosphere. Consider the region (city, rural, suburb), inside surroundings (type of building, kind of furniture, color of the walls), smells, the season, the color of the sky, and the weather. The more detailed the setting, the more it comes to life.

CHARACTERS

These can be real people, pretend people, animals, made-up creatures (monsters, goblins, witches, fairies), and inanimate objects with human characteristics (talking trucks, trees that hug). Consider personality, physical characteristics, their pasts, the conflicts and problems they face, who and what they love, what they wear, whether they change over the course of the story, what motivates them, and their shortcomings.

PLOT

The basic elements of plot:

INTRODUCTION: Of characters, setting, and the events that give rise to a conflict.

RISING ACTION: The furthering of that conflict.

CLIMAX: The turning point in the story — its most suspenseful and intense part.

FALLING ACTION: How the conflict is resolved.

RESOLUTION: Characters realize the implications the conflict has on their lives and come to terms with what has happened. For example, characters make changes, learn lessons, work harder, teach others, spread the word, become more careful, and so forth.

CONFLICT

The forces don't have to be two characters. A character can struggle with the weather, bad luck, his past, the law, traditions, memories, a disability, feelings from within: the list goes on. In addition, a story can have multiple conflicts! External conflicts are struggles characters have with forces outside of themselves, and internal conflicts are struggles characters have with themselves.

THEME

A story can have multiple themes. Some examples:

- Friends make life more interesting.
- Courage comes in many forms.
- Appearances can be deceiving.
- Honesty is the best policy.

THE STORY

As children are ready to learn about the framework of storytelling, share these elements with them.

SETTING

Where the story takes place.

CHARACTERS

Who the story's about. (It doesn't have to be a person!)

PLOT

What happens in the story — often, a conflict and its resolution.

CONFLICT

A struggle between two (or more!) forces in a story.

THEME

A main insight of the story.

Beginning, Middle, End

This story-prompt game provides a spontaneous way to experiment with developing the framework for a story. Children use three random story prompts to create a beginning, a middle, and an end for their stories. It may be some children's first experience actively planning and structuring a story.

HOW TO MAKE

TIME
To make: **1 hour**

AGES
To make: **7+**
To use: **7+**

PLAYERS
1+

MATERIALS
➤ **scissors**
➤ **scrap paper**
➤ **pencils**
➤ **3 paper envelopes (bought or made with the template on page 132)**
➤ **alphabet stamps (optional)**
➤ **fine-tip marker**
➤ **paper**

1. Cut the scrap paper into slightly smaller than 3" squares. Try to make a minimum of 45 squares; the more you make, the more varied your story possibilities will be. Don't put too much initial pressure on your-selves to produce, as you can always add new story-prompt squares to your collection. Just do what feels manageable and fun. Set aside.

2. Using the template on page 132, make three envelopes. Or have your children creatively decorate three store-bought envelopes, and then clearly write or stamp BEGINNING on one, MIDDLE on the next, and END on the third. Children will store their story-prompt squares in these envelopes.

3. To create the content for the squares, spend time with your young story-tellers composing a long list of story prompts. Put your heads together to think of as many scenarios, character descriptions, settings, things, feel-ings, and plot points as possible (see Story Sparks, page 50, for ideas). Just when you think you can't come up with another idea, encourage yourself and your children to think of just a few more.

4. Once your list is long and juicy, use fine-tip markers to write a prompt on each of the paper squares.

   The result will be a big messy pile of story-prompt squares in desper-ate need of some organization. Dive in with your children and divide the big pile into three relatively even, tidy stacks. Don't think about any particular order or grouping. Put one pile of prompts into each of the envelopes.

HOW TO PLAY

What I love about this exercise is that it challenges creative minds to develop a story within a preexisting structure. Tricky! Chances are your children will come up with stories they would never have thought of otherwise. Let's say someone gets bird feeder, wrench, *and* snowy mountains. *What's her next move?*

1. Set one sheet of blank paper and the three envelopes on the table. A child chooses a square from the BEGINNING envelope and tapes it in the top-left corner of the paper. Next, she chooses a square from the MIDDLE envelope, and then she selects one from the END envelope, taping the squares in order across the top of the page. Now she has three important details about the beginning, middle, and end of her story.

   These details shouldn't be all spent in the beginning of the story; they are meant to anchor and frame the story, providing a basic structure.

2. If a child is planning to write a more elaborate story, encourage him to spend some time taking notes on the rest of the story. In what context will he use the details? How will the three chosen details relate? What happens in between? Will there be conflict? Once he has made notes, he can use them to write his story. If he wants to use his three prompts for a more off-the-cuff storytelling session, scrap the notes and encourage him to go for it.

3. Educators and families can turn this into a group activity. One person chooses three story prompts and tapes them to the paper. Every person in the group uses the same three sequential prompts to write a story. Once all group members are finished, each person has the opportunity to read her story aloud. Be prepared to be endlessly inspired when you hear what others have created with the same material.

other **neat** things

>> Have a child do this exercise on her own, then ask someone to guess which three aspects of the story were the selected prompts.

>> After a story is written or told, children can draw three pictures that depict the three prompts.

>> Once a child has used his sequential prompts, ask him to put them in reverse order and try again.

Story Grab Bag

With its mixture of images, ideas, numbers, and words, this is the most versatile of all the Story Starters. With this project, you'll create an endless supply of inspiration that children can tap in to at any time. Use this grab bag to begin a story, to build a framework for a story, or to facilitate community storytelling.

TIME
To make: **At least 1 hour**

AGES
To make: **5+**
To use: **5+**

PLAYERS
1+

MATERIALS
- pages from old magazines
- scissors
- stamps and ink pads
- glue stick
- cardstock
- bone folder
- Mod Podge and foam brush (optional)
- an empty bag or box with a lid

I used story grab bags when I taught creative writing at a high school. The kids loved that it felt like a game, and the process led to unique and fascinating stories. I tend to dip into a bag when I'm stuck with my own creative writing, and my kids and students love to spin tales based on what pops out of the bag.

HOW TO MAKE

1. Search through magazines, maps, catalogs, and personal drawings for material, choosing anything that might make a story interesting: words, numbers, illustrations, or photographs. When you find a

picture that's intriguing or curious, neatly cut it out, following the contour of the image. This is a perfect way for children to participate, and in the process of choosing, you'll get to see the kinds of images that interest them. As you're searching, if you think of an image that you're unable to find in your materials, look online in an open-source-photograph website for images (see Online Shops, page 131). You can also draw, stamp, or paint your own version of the image.

2. Gather your neatly trimmed images into a tidy stack. Using the glue stick, coat a piece of cardstock with a thin layer of glue, then lay as many images as will fit onto the glue-coated paper. Use your fingers and a bone folder to smooth out air bubbles and wrinkles. Repeat the gluing and pressing step until all of the images are glued flat onto cardstock, then set aside to dry. This first gluing step will ensure that the images are affixed to the cardstock smoothly and neatly.

TEACHING TIP Sort the prompts into groups and prepackage them in envelopes. Give the same group of prompts to several students, and then share the resulting stories.

other neat ideas

≫ Put Velcro on the back of the prompts and stick some on a felt board as a way to display stories and storytelling.

≫ Sort the prompts into thematic groups (love, animals, seasons, nature, strength, for example) for a more focused kind of storytelling.

≫ Take a Story Grab Bag along on car rides and pass it around for an on-the-go group story-telling game.

≫ Use the Story Sparks word lists (page 50) to fill a grab bag instead of (or in addition to) images.

3. With the foam brush, add a layer of Mod Podge to the top surface to give the images a nice, thick, substantial, clear coating. (If you decide not to use Mod Podge, skip to step 4.) Set on dry cloth and let dry overnight. This Mod Podge step will leave the images feeling more substantial.

4. Once the sheets with the images are fully dry, neatly cut out the images and put into the bag.

HOW TO USE
For Individual Storytelling

Ask a child to choose five Story Starters from the grab bag, and have her use those five ideas to build a story.

Younger children can tell a stream-of-consciousness sort of story, which an adult can record in a notebook. Older children can use the Story Starters to frame a story by sorting the ideas and strategically placing them at different points of the tale.

For Group Storytelling

With the children sitting in a circle, the first storyteller chooses something from the grab bag and begins the story. Each child takes a turn selecting and telling, while an adult records the story as it unfolds. In my workshops, we like to read the completed story after we've finished creating it; it's a way to celebrate the story we've made together.

another neat idea
>> Use alphabet stamps to label images for young readers.

These Are the Stories in My Neighborhood

This colorful, fanciful project asks children to imagine the people and families who live inside the houses in a pretend neighborhood. Once the children have filled their stamped houses with characters, furniture, food, and other details, they will be inspired to begin telling stories about the folks who live inside.

TIME
To make: **2–3 hours**

AGES
To make: **5+**

To use: **5+**

PLAYERS
1+

HOW TO MAKE

1. To make the base for the house stamp, find a piece of scrap wood that will be big enough and use sandpaper to smooth any sharp edges.

2. On the craft foam sheet, use a pencil and ruler to draw a triangle with a base of 4" and a square or rectangle with 4" sides. With a sharp scissors

MATERIALS

- pieces of scrap wood at least 3" × 5" (for the base for the house stamp)
- sandpaper
- pencil
- ruler
- adhesive-backed craft foam sheets
- scissors
- pigment-colored ink pads
- blank paper
- damp cloth
- black art pens
- colored pencils
- colored paper
- glue stick

and a steady hand, cut out the triangle and the square. Embrace any imperfections that arise; these will just make the house seem original and loved.

3. Peel off the paper on the back of the square, and firmly press the craft foam onto the wood base. Leaving a thin gap above the square, peel the paper from the triangle and press it onto the wood base to form a roof.

4. To use your stamp, hold the ink pad in one hand and the stamp in the other and gently dab the ink pad onto the surface to coat it with ink. Apply a thin, even layer of ink onto the square, then do the same with the triangle but with different-colored ink. Place the stamp face-down on a sheet of blank paper, press firmly with the palm of your hand, and lift it away to reveal the house. Use a damp cloth to wipe the stamp clean.

5. Apply different ink colors and stamp another house right next to the first. Repeat until you have as long a neighborhood street as you want.

Start with scrap wood.

Add shapes cut
from craft foam.

Notice the thin gap between
the roof and the house?
This gives the print definition.

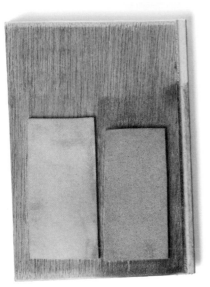

Use different colored ink pads.

Your neighborhood!

6. Once the neighborhood is dry, your children can fill the houses with characters, furniture, food, and more. Have them use black art pens and colored pencils to add details, and scissors, colored paper, and glue to make additions to the buildings. Once their neighborhood is complete, ask them to tell you the story about all of the folks who live there.

other neat ideas

>> Make a neighborhood that reflects a certain season or weather pattern (snow, leaves, spring flowers, wind).

>> Create different styles of homes and buildings with different craft foam shapes. Experiment with semicircle and trapezoidal roofs.

>> Turn some neighborhoods into greeting cards to send to friends and family.

TEACHING TIP Create one neighborhood template, and then make color photocopies of it to hand out to your students over the course of a year.

GROUP STORYTELLING

Group storytelling can feel magical and inspiring for children — and it helps them cultivate friend-ships and appreciate other people's ideas. Often it leads to laughter, excitement, and camaraderie. As children tell a collective story, a mutual desire arises: they want the best for their story. In this context, they tend to value other children's unique contributions and you'll see them praising and applauding each other's efforts.

It's natural, though, for some people to feel frus-trated with collaborative storytelling, as it requires giving up control of a story's trajectory. In this case, it is good to remind children that it is very *different* from telling your own story. Yes, one person doesn't make all of the decisions, but this is what makes things interesting. For most children, sticking it out and engaging in the game from beginning to end will be enough to win them over. Adaptability and resilience are so important for children of all ages to practice, and learning to share their creative experiences with their peers is the basis for cooperative learning. In the end, the group story is more than a story — it's a valuable community-building exercise.

Magnetic Story Board

TIME
To make: 2–3 hands-on hours

AGES
To make: 5+

To use: 3+

PLAYERS
2+

MATERIALS
- sandpaper
- wood or plywood board approximately 12" × 18"
- paintbrushes
- magnetic primer paint (see Materials, page 129)
- topcoat paint
- metal picture hanger hardware
- magazines, catalogs, maps, drawings
- scissors
- glue stick
- cardstock or cereal-box panel
- bone folder
- Mod Podge and foam brush (optional)
- round ¾" magnets (see Materials, page 129)
- hot-glue gun with glue sticks or strong craft glue

Use the Magnetic Story Board to facilitate group storytelling games. Prop the board against a wall or hang it on a nail, and place the handmade magnets on the board so children can create original stories whenever they feel inspired.

HOW TO MAKE

1. To make the magnetic board: With the sandpaper, smooth the edges and surfaces of the wooden board. Dust off the wooden bits. Coat one surface of the board with the magnetic primer paint, then allow the magnetic layer to dry completely. Once the paint is dry, coat it with a layer of regular paint in any color you choose. Attach the metal picture hanger to the back of the board.

2. To make the magnets: Search through magazines, maps, catalogs, dilapidated books, and personal drawings for material. Look for anything that might make a story interesting: words, numbers, illustrations, photographs. When you find pictures that seem intriguing or curious, neatly cut them out following the contour of the images. This is a perfect way for your children to participate, and in the process of making selections, you'll get to see the kinds of images that interest them. As you're searching, if you think of an image that you're unable to find in your materials, look online in an open-source-photograph website (see Online Shops, page 131). Or consider drawing or painting your own version of the image.

3. Gather your neatly trimmed images into a tidy stack. Using the glue stick, coat a piece of cardstock with a thin layer of glue, then lay as many images as will fit onto the glue-coated paper. Use your fingers and a bone folder to smooth out any air bubbles and wrinkles.

4. Repeat the gluing and pressing step until all of the images are glued flat onto multiple sheets of cardstock, then set them aside to dry.

5. Dip the foam brush into the Mod Podge, and apply a thin, even coat to the top surface of all of the images. Let dry overnight. This Mod Podge step will protect the images and leave them feeling more substantial. (If you decide not to use Mod Podge, skip to step 6.)

6. Once the sheets with the images are fully dry, cut around the images; set aside.

7. Flip the images over and use hot glue to apply the round magnets to the back. Strong craft glue can be used in lieu of a hot-glue gun. Repeat this step for all of the images.

HOW TO USE

The first person in the group places a magnet on the board and begins the story, then chooses another magnet for the board. The second person finds a way to incorporate the newest magnet into the story, and then leaves a magnet for the next person to incorporate. This goes on until the story is complete or until each person has had a turn.

Safety note: Children must be over 3 to play with magnets.

other neat ideas

» Make a mini board and a mini set of magnets as a travel set, and use on the road.

» Make some story-magnet sets to give to friends.

» Stick the story magnets on the refrigerator for additional storytelling fun.

» Children can use the board to plan a story by moving characters and objects until they discover how all of the different parts of the story fit together.

Story Sparks

If you or your children are stuck and feel at a loss for a setting or character-description detail, Story Sparks are a great way to be quickly inspired. You can use all of these ideas for impromptu storytelling or for inspiration as you make the storytelling crafts and projects in this book. Use any of these words (or create a list of your own) to make another version of the Story Grab Bag (page 40).

One day far far away a boy named turned magicaly into a ogre by old warty green with 2 warts her eyes And one on the tip

WHO

CHOOSE A CHARACTER

- ○ elf
- ○ farmer
- ○ family of birds
- ○ superhero
- ○ dolphin
- ○ vegetable truck driver
- ○ tree
- ○ monster
- ○ baby or toddler
- ○ rock star
- ○ mermaid
- ○ house*
- ○ tornado
- ○ carnival worker
- ○ soldier
- ○ lizard
- ○ astronaut
- ○ deep-sea diver
- ○ wise elder
- ○ tour guide
- ○ 19th-century shop owner
- ○ artist

WHAT ARE THEY LIKE?

- ○ impish
- ○ frightened
- ○ angry
- ○ curious
- ○ shy
- ○ jealous
- ○ creepy
- ○ talkative
- ○ snobbish
- ○ cursed
- ○ messy
- ○ creative
- ○ nurturing
- ○ regretful
- ○ rebellious
- ○ sensible
- ○ loud
- ○ inspiring
- ○ forgiving
- ○ adventurous
- ○ successful
- ○ menacing
- ○ lucky
- ○ sensitive

WHERE

CHOOSE A PLACE

- ○ train
- ○ house*
- ○ theater
- ○ moon
- ○ closet
- ○ boat
- ○ castle
- ○ beehive
- ○ restaurant
- ○ cave
- ○ North Pole
- ○ radio station
- ○ airport
- ○ carnival
- ○ fairy house
- ○ playground
- ○ rooftop
- ○ museum
- ○ campground
- ○ under the bed
- ○ mountaintop
- ○ school

WHAT IS IT LIKE?

- ○ musty
- ○ in the future
- ○ in the past
- ○ scorching
- ○ buggy
- ○ cold
- ○ tranquil
- ○ spooky
- ○ steep
- ○ protected
- ○ dangerous
- ○ magical
- ○ luxurious
- ○ messy
- ○ mysterious
- ○ lush
- ○ enchanted
- ○ dreadful
- ○ spectacular
- ○ crooked
- ○ glowing
- ○ polluted

 Yes, a house can be a character in a story or, of course, the setting.

CHOOSE A THING

- ○ microphone
- ○ sandwich
- ○ sleeping bag
- ○ seashells
- ○ magic flute
- ○ invisible ink
- ○ postcard
- ○ map
- ○ walking stick
- ○ disguise
- ○ ring
- ○ poison ivy
- ○ anthill
- ○ crystals
- ○ fishing pole
- ○ bicycle
- ○ beads
- ○ truck
- ○ Tarot cards
- ○ wagon
- ○ ball
- ○ disguise
- ○ skateboard
- ○ camera

CHOOSE AN EVENT

- ○ a vacation
- ○ a birth
- ○ a party
- ○ a walk in the woods
- ○ an ocean swim
- ○ a birthday
- ○ a day at the fair
- ○ a graduation
- ○ a holiday
- ○ a bike ride
- ○ a picnic
- ○ the Olympics
- ○ a day at the park
- ○ the first day of school
- ○ a boat ride
- ○ going camping
- ○ a marathon
- ○ going to a movie
- ○ planting a garden
- ○ a reunion
- ○ a move

WHEN

CHOOSE A TIME

- ○ far in the future
- ○ one hour from now
- ○ when the dinosaurs roamed
- ○ before cars
- ○ when you were a baby
- ○ during the reign of Queen Elizabeth I
- ○ when you're in college
- ○ before computers
- ○ when your grandmother was five
- ○ during the Roaring 20s
- ○ during the Italian Renaissance

WHY

DO YOU HAVE A PROBLEM?

- something gets lost
- someone is put under a spell
- something is broken
- a misunder-standing
- disappointment
- someone breaks a promise
- homesickness
- a lie is told
- someone gets hurt
- someone has a nightmare
- someone is sick
- a mean person
- something is stolen

HOW WILL YOU SOLVE IT?

- by using magic
- by remembering past lessons
- by taking a risk
- by finding hidden treasure
- by consulting ancient tomes
- by asking for help
- by using the right tool
- a stranger has an idea
- a new character comes to town
- a dream reveals a clue
- characters work together
- a loyal friend helps
- a memory resurfaces

TRY THESE . . .

- She hid the envelope in a book at the bottom of a drawer in her desk where she knew nobody would find it . . .

- He drew a little star next to one of the names on the list. He must remember that man's name . . .

- The whole morning, while the other campers were canoeing, he cried into his pillow . . .

- She wondered what was around the next bend on this dark and twisty road. They had been walking for hours . . .

- He was digging in the center of the garden when his trowel hit something hard . . .

- Curiosity got the best of him, and he decided to get into the car and drive over to learn more for himself . . .

- The airplane was about to take off. She was feeling sad to leave her friends and family, but excited about her new adventure . . .

- Caves are dangerous, he had always thought. Yet here he was, about to go deep into the earth with only his head-light and some friends to guide him.

- The lightning crashed and the house went dark . . .

- He was wasting time at the store when he noticed two people looking at him strangely . . .

... when they got to the top of the hill, they found a magical place ...

2 story evolution

deepen and expand your stories

> A rock pile ceases to be a rock pile the moment a single man contemplates it, bearing within him the image of a cathedral.
>
> — ANTOINE DE SAINT-EXUPÉRY

Children tell stories all day long. Listen and you'll hear them muttered in between bites of cereal or perhaps whispered just before nodding off. Look and you'll see them interpreted in their stacks of drawings or piled into mountains and castles in the sandbox. They are threaded through a child's consciousness and are often the basis for how he views and interacts with his world.

The projects in this chapter present ways to encourage and facilitate children's existing relationship with stories. Tailor these activities to their interests, and they will welcome undiscovered lands and unfamiliar characters into their own familiar world.

→ Carry a notepad and pencil everywhere.

Portable Projects

These projects are intentionally portable so that the creative process doesn't have to stop because of your busy schedule. Bring them along to the waiting room at the dentist, on a car trip, to Nana's house, to the seaside motel, or to a sibling's soccer practice. Bring them along on family or school trips, and see how scenery changes and travel can influence storytelling. Encourage children to carry a notepad and pencil everywhere, and bring along your own notebook to record for the young storytellers who can't yet write their tales.

Story Stones

Stones covered with images create unique and intriguing storytelling toys. They can be used just about anywhere for a quick, fun, creative game. But beware; they're addictive! Once they make one, your children won't stop thinking of additions for their collection.

TIME
To make: **At least 1 hour**

AGES
To make: **5+**
(with adult help)

To use: **3+**

PLAYERS
1+

MATERIALS
➤ **smooth stones of all shapes and sizes**
➤ **small scrub brush**
➤ **towel**
➤ **pencil and paper**
➤ **fabric pencil**
➤ **bits of fabric and paper scraps**
➤ **scissors**
➤ **Mod Podge**
➤ **foam brush**
➤ **⅛" hole punch**
➤ **string**
➤ **small seeds (poppy, sesame)**
➤ **toothpick or Q-tip**
➤ **newspaper or wax paper**

HOW TO MAKE

1. To clean the stones, put them in a sink, fill the sink with water, and have someone who loves to play with water scrub each one with a brush. Once all of the stones are rinsed, place them on a towel in a warm spot to dry.

2. Enlist children to help design the different characters and objects for the stones, and make sketches or lists to help you remember what you want to create. You can also engage in a free-form creative process in which you decide what to make next while in the process of creating.

3. Using a fabric pencil, draw on your favorite fabric or paper the shapes that make up each character or object. Try drawing different parts of the shape onto different papers

NOTES ON THE SEARCH FOR STONES

I like to collect throughout the year, so I don't have to worry about running out of stones when the ground is buried under layers of crusty snow. Try to find a variety of shapes and sizes to ensure that you have many options. The ideal size and shape is a round or oval stone averaging 1½" to 2½" in both height and width. A smooth and flat surface is easier to work with than are rough or jagged surfaces. Search in forests, your backyard, the beach, meadows, lakes, ponds, and rivers.

A few years back, I found a beach where, for miles and miles, there were layers of small, smooth stones. The only containers I had on hand were two cloth grocery bags, and I filled them with stones — and I've gone back since to replenish my supply. It's nice to conduct a purposeful stone search, but be sure to keep your eyes peeled for stones when you aren't intentionally looking for them. After making a bunch of Story Stones, you'll soon be able to quickly size up stones for their potential. Leah and Hazel often join in and run to me with "the perfect" stone or toss a jagged stone aside while muttering "Nope."

CREATING
A FIGURE

Cover with Mod Podge.

and fabrics to make a collaged image. This will give you more control over the way it looks in the end and enables you to experiment with a variety of colors and textures. Carefully cut out each piece.

4. Find a stone that works well with one of your character designs, and coat it with a thin layer of Mod Podge. Set the first shape from your design on the stone and coat with more Mod Podge. Use your fingertips to rearrange the design so that it is positioned just right. Smooth out any wrinkles or air bubbles.

Continue adding the pieces until the design is complete. Add circles of hole-punched paper, bits of string, even small seeds to create tiny details such as eyes, flowers, leaves, and food.

5. Put one last coat of Mod Podge over the finished design. It is very important that a layer of Mod Podge cover all of the design; use a toothpick or Q-tip to cover any of the tiny details or to pop any air bubbles. At this point, the Mod Podge will be white and opaque, which means it will be difficult to see your designs. Don't fret! It will dry clear and smooth.

It isn't necessary to coat the bottom of the stone with Mod Podge, and in fact, doing so will make it more difficult to dry the stones because unwanted bits of paper might attach to it.

TEACHING TIP For early-childhood educators, foreign-language teachers, and developmental specialists, the Story Stones are a creative way to teach vocabulary.

6. Set the Story Stones on a piece of newspaper or wax paper to dry. Once the first layer is dry, you may want to apply a second coat of Mod Podge to give it extra protection. Let the stones dry fully; the top layer should feel completely hard — not tacky — before play begins.

HOW TO USE

1. Encourage children to use the stones for imaginative, dramatic play in the same way they would use small dolls and toy figurines.

2. The stones can be used outside, in a dollhouse, on a table or play mat, or in the car. To keep them in tip-top shape, avoid splashing them or submerging them in water or another liquid.

3. Make sets of stones and store them in small bags, in boxes, or even in socks to preserve your collections for future play.

other **neat** ideas

>> Give Story Stones as small gifts or party favors.

>> Create thematic sets of stones: picnic, carnival, ocean, around the house, schooltime.

>> For younger children, 3+ years, invite them to just glue fabric and paper scraps onto the stones. These more abstract collage stones can become part of the storytelling process but don't require specific cutting and placement skills.

Coat the top of the stone with Mod Podge, and then place the fabric.

Paint Mod Podge over all fabric.

Finished!

Traveling Puppet Theater

You can use this portable storytelling theater with puppets anywhere. With it, children may control the entire storytelling process, directing all the action, staging, and character placement. Characters and objects can be moved forward and backward on the backdrop as part of the story performance.

TIME
To make: **3–4 hours**

AGES
To make: **5+**
To use: **3+**

PLAYERS
1+

MATERIALS
➤ an empty cereal box or pieces of cardboard
➤ scissors
➤ pencil
➤ craft paint
➤ blank paper
➤ felt markers
➤ catalogs and magazines
➤ craft glue
➤ Mod Podge and foam brush
➤ wide tongue depressors (a.k.a. "craft sticks")
➤ wooden clothespins
➤ books
➤ ruler
➤ craft knife
➤ pencil

HOW TO MAKE

1. To make the theater stage, cut the front and back panels from the cereal box, using the folds of the box as guidelines for cutting as straight as possible.

2. With a pencil, draw a horizon line on the unprinted side of one of the panels. Consider the natural lines of a landscape as you place this line. If you'd like, sketch in some hills and valleys or perhaps a flat desert.

3. Once you are satisfied with the placement of the horizon line, paint the area above it as desired, with sky, buildings, or water. Allow to dry, then paint the section below the line, with perhaps a grassy hill, a sandy beach, the surface of the moon, or the ocean.

4. Select or draw puppet images. To create images for the characters and any other objects or props, draw them on a sheet of paper with markers, glue collage materials, or select images from magazines and catalogs. Cut out each image.

5. With the foam brush, coat the unprinted side of another cereal-box panel with a thin layer of Mod Podge. Place the cut-out images faceup on the panel and coat with another layer of Mod Podge, using your fingertips to smooth out any air bubbles or wrinkles. Allow to dry overnight.

6. To make the puppets, cut out each image on the cardboard. Apply craft glue to the back of each image and attach it to the top of a craft stick, with the image extending just beyond the top of the stick. Lay all the glued sticks on a piece of paper, then clamp each stick with a clothespin. (Several heavy books will also work.) Once dry, it may be helpful to keep a pile of books on them overnight to ensure that they remain flat.

7. To cut a slot in the theater stage, using a ruler, draw two straight lines on the back of the painted theater stage, each about 3" long, for the puppets to poke through and move. Make one on the left part of the panel and another on the right. You don't want them to be too long, but you do want to make them long enough for two puppets to fit into one slot. Making one slot a little higher than the other adds some depth and is good for imaginative play. Cut the slits with a craft knife.

Safety Note: Take special care with the craft knife. Adults need to help with this step and supervise older children.

HOW TO USE

Once the puppets are dry and flattened, slide them through the slots and you're ready to start telling stories. Create a variety of backdrops, so the characters can move to different places, times, and climates: under the sea, in the jungle, on an eighteenth-century farm, in a city, on the moon, or at the beach. The creative options are endless!

See pages 136–139 for fun puppets to copy and cut out. And at the end of the book you'll find two puppet theaters!

other **neat ideas**

>> Give the puppets as small gifts or party favors.

>> A perk for parents is this theater's compact size, which makes the sets conducive to car trips and train rides. Teachers will also appreciate that they fit nicely in small bags and folders.

>> Have your child make a classroom backdrop with student puppets as an end-of-year gift to a beloved teacher. The teacher can look like the child's teacher!

Memory Cards

These colorful, captivating cards can be used to slowly and comprehensively tell the story of a special and important memory. As each card is presented, the child tells a bit of the story as she explains the circumstances surrounding the visual, as well as the significance behind it.

TIME
To make: **2–3 hours**

AGES
To make: **5+**

To use: **3+**

PLAYERS
1+

MATERIALS
- ➤ **scissors**
- ➤ **cereal-box panels**
- ➤ **corner-rounding punch (optional, see Materials, page 129)**
- ➤ **colorful scrap paper for collage**
- ➤ **Mod Podge**
- ➤ **foam brush**
- ➤ **scissors**
- ➤ **craft knife (for cutting small details)**
- ➤ **hole punch (optional)**
- ➤ **assorted decorative punches (optional)**

HOW TO MAKE

1. Spend time with your child deciding which memory she would like to retell.

2. Once the two of you have decided, think of eight (fewer or more is fine) specific visual details from the memory. Choosing these details is fun, but it also provides practice in deciphering the most special, important, or salient details of a story. Learning to know what to include in a story and what to leave out is an important storytelling skill, and here the child is asked to use a few essential details to act as the backbone of the story.

3. Cut eight 3" × 4" rectangles out of the cereal box panels. If you'd like, give the cards rounded edges by punching each corner with the corner-rounding punch. For me, giving the cards rounded corners helps them to look finished and gives them a sense of belonging together.

4. To create collaged visuals for each of the eight details, use scissors, a craft knife, and decorative punches to cut shapes out of different colors, patterns, and textures. The simple, colorful collages will pop against the soft matte brown of the cereal-box cards.

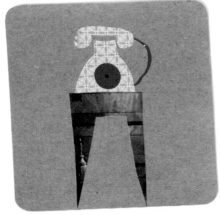

5. To affix the collages, with the foam brush, coat each card with a thin layer of Mod Podge. Then, carefully apply the collage pieces to the cards and gently cover with another layer of Mod Podge. Use your fingertips to press and smooth away any air bubbles or wrinkles.

6. Set aside to dry. Once they are fully dry, keep them flat by placing a heavy book on top of them and leave overnight.

HOW TO USE

Have children shuffle the cards, and then spend time arranging them in the correct order while telling the full story of the memory.

other **neat** ideas

» Display a set of Memory Cards on a shelf in your living space, and they will serve as a conversation spark.

» Shuffle together a few sets of Memory Cards, and have children sift through the pile to determine which cards go with which memory.

» Frame some of the Memory Cards, together or separately, to hang on a wall or give to a loved one.

» Use this technique to make story cards for imaginary tales.

When we arrived at Aunt Susan and Uncle Claude's beach cottage, they gave us each a pinwheel to play with.

One Labor Day weekend, our family left early in the morning and drove to the Connecticut Sound, where we went on a ferry ride. After dinner in Greenport, New York, we took the ferry home and arrived, sleepily, at our door at midnight. When we awoke the next morning, it felt like a long, sea-salty dream, so Leah and I decided to preserve the vacation with Memory Cards. Our eight visual details were the ferry; a pinwheel; a small, sandy beach; a beach filled with stones (perfect for Story Stones); a fish; a peach; the vibrant village of Greenport; and some colorful buoys that were hanging on a wall. Each detail is connected to a very special part of the day. Here, we've pasted on the back of each card our written descriptions (and you can see what cardboard we salvaged!).

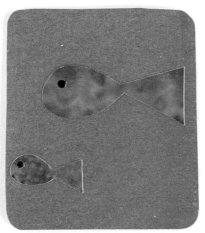

We played at the beach at the end of the path. It had smooth sand and beautiful shells.

We brought peach cobbler to share with family

On the way back to the ferryboat, we walked on the streets of the bustling, merry seaside town.

Story Mat

This mat will instantly turn a bare floor into a faraway land where characters can travel in search of magic, adventures, or friendship. An elaborate mat can be exciting for children, but don't feel pressured to make it complex and full; a simple mat will provide hours of storytelling fun. In fact, I often create a simple mat with a grassy hill, some water, and a mountain, and I find that the stories that come from it are as fascinating as those from the mats with volcanoes, pirate ships, fairy houses, and castles.

TIME
To make: **3 hours**

AGES
To make: **6+**

To use: **3+**

PLAYERS
1+

HOW TO MAKE

1. To prepare your fabric, cut it to desired play-mat size. I like 30" × 24", but you can make it bigger or smaller depending on your vision. Don't worry about the unfinished edges. If you'd like, you can finish it with a simple hem or bias tape.

2. Use the fabric pencil to draw landscape designs on the mat. You can create a horizon line and incorporate both sky and earth or take a bird's-eye view. Whatever your perspective, draw a variety of details such as a river, a lake, bushes, rows of corn, paths, rocks, and a mountain.

MATERIALS

- 1 yard of thick, neutral-colored fabric, such as canvas or duck
- scissors
- needle and thread or bias tape (optional)
- fabric pencil
- fabric paint (craft paint works if you don't plan to wash the mat)
- objects for print making (pencil erasers, sponge pieces, adhesive-backed craft foam, and wooden blocks)
- felt and cotton fabric scraps
- embroidery needle and floss

If you're stuck on how to draw the elements, use purchased stencils to make more intricate images like a castle, a car, and a house.

3. Mix a variety of bright paint colors, then fill in the pencil lines. As the paint is drying, look around your house for found objects to use to stamp designs or textures on your mat. Use bits of rounded sponge to create water texture. Cut adhesive-backed craft foam into small triangles and attach to a small block of wood to stamp triangular trees. A pencil eraser top dipped lightly in paint can create little patches of flowers, apples on a tree, even fireflies.

4. To add more textural details, cut out shapes from fabric with different patterns and finishes; quilter's cotton, calico, felt, and flannel are good materials. Use embroidery thread and a simple running stitch to attach these shapes to the cloth. Fabric is great for creating mountains, treetops, sailboats, houses, clouds, and gardens. Let your imagination guide you!

5. Allow the mat to dry fully before playing with it.

HOW TO USE

Put the mat on the floor, along with Story Stones (page 57), models, or other character figures your children like to play with, and watch the storytelling begin.

other neat ideas

>> Create a wide range of habitats for your Story Mat: the moon, a desert, under the sea, the beach, a zoo, a highway, a forest, a city, a snowstorm with a frozen lake, or a magical land.

>> Fold up the mat, pack it flat in a suitcase, and bring it along on your travels. Hotel rooms and tents can be transformed into imaginary lands.

>> Make a mat that looks like a theater with a stage, spotlight, and curtain.

Any small character can become a Broadway star!

>> Encourage your child to bring his Story Mat outside. Pinecones, pebbles, pine needles, leaves, and seeds can be transformed into pretend characters.

STORY EVOLUTION

Storytelling Jar

Think of it as a storytelling terrarium. Children enjoy using the Storytelling Jar to inspire their imagination and tell stories about its inhabitants. Encourage children to change the Story Stones in order to create new and different stories. Put one on a desk or table as inspiration for a young writer. The experience of planning for and actually making the jar is fun and highly imaginative.

TIME
To make: 1½–2 hours

AGES
To make: 5+ (with the help of an adult)

To use: 3+

PLAYERS
1+

MATERIALS
- 9" diameter lid or circular stencil
- marker
- ¼ yard green felt
- scissors
- needle and thread
- stuffing
- glass jar (dill pickle or applesauce size)
- fabric glue
- hole punch
- paper scraps
- sharp knife
- a button
- masking tape
- Story Stones (page 57)

HOW TO MAKE

1. Draw or trace a circle with a diameter of 9" onto the green felt. It's great if you happen to have an 9" circle stencil, but if not, don't fret; use a lid or cake pan. If you end up drawing the circle freehand, try to make it as symmetrical as possible.

2. Cut out the circle, then sew a loose running stitch around its entire circumference.

3. Once stitching is in place, tug the thread gently to create a little pocket, then fill it with stuffing. After it's stuffed, give the thread a harder tug. This should create a little stuffed-felt mound. When you're happy with the shape and size of the grassy mound, secure the tuft by passing a needle through the edges of the circle a few times. Be sure to retain the tension on the thread so the circle remains cinched, and then after passing the needle through two edges of the circle, tightly double-knot the thread. This green-felt mound will be the grassy hill at the bottom of the jar.

4. Trace the bottom of the glass jar onto a different piece of green felt, and cut out the circle. Before putting the hill inside the jar, place this green felt circle at the bottom of the jar to fill in the areas where light filters through. Use a dot of glue under the felt circle to be sure it stays in place. Place the grassy hill on top of the felt circle. Use your hands to adjust the stuffing and shape to resemble a grassy hill.

5. Use the hole punch to create tiny felt and paper "flowers," and secure them on the hill with tiny, tiny dabs of fabric glue. I have an old hole punch that I reserve for felt. It tends to punch out only half of a circle, but I use my small, sharp scissors to help it along. Be creative! You can also cut tiny flower shapes from fabric. Adorn your hill with whatever strikes your fancy.

6. Cut a tiny hot air balloon out of paper. Other flying options: airplane, squirrel, bat, bee, helicopter, bird, skydiver, blimp. Use a needle and thread to create a hanging loop off the top of the balloon.

7. Using a sharp knife, an adult carefully punches a hole in the lid of the jar. Do your best to bend the edges over so they aren't sharp. Feed the balloon thread up through the lid's hole; tie the outer ends of the thread to a button to keep it from falling through. Protect small hands with masking tape over the sharp edges inside the lid.

8. Set Story Stones (characters or objects) onto the hill to create a variety of storytelling situations.

other neat ideas

>> Give a Storytelling Jar as a gift to a teacher or friend.

>> Add trees, a nest with eggs, or a picnic blanket to the hill. String some vines, or hang the sun, moon, and stars.

>> Encourage your child to write a small poem about the inhabitants of the jar and tape it to the inside, so the words can be seen from the outside. Change the poem when new inspiration strikes.

>> Make a jar for every season. Use sparkly white glitter for winter.

Storybook

A blank Storybook is a great companion for all storytelling crafts and activities. Encourage children to record their stories, so they can remember and retell them in years to come. Children can use collage materials to decorate it with an inspiring design tailored just for them.

TIME
To make: **2 hours**

AGES
To make: **5+**

To use: **5+**

PLAYERS
1+

MATERIALS
- cardstock
- ruler
- bone folder
- blank lightweight paper
- scissors
- pencil
- cutting board
- nail (or awl)
- small hammer
- embroidery needle
- embroidery floss or waxed-linen binding floss
- corner-rounding punch (optional, see Materials on page 129)

HOW TO MAKE

1. Decide what size the book will be. Does your child want a pocket-size book? Wallet-size? Larger? Determine the functionality and size of the book. Trim the cardstock to size accordingly, using the bone folder to crease it down the center, then set it aside. This is the cover.

2. Decide how many pages should be in the book by multiplying the number of sheets of paper by 4. For example, if you use 3 sheets of paper, the book will have 12 blank pages.

3. To ensure that the paper doesn't stick out of the book, measure the lightweight paper so that it is about ¼" smaller than the cover. Cut it to size, and use the bone folder to make a sharp crease down the center of each page.

4. With the cardstock open on the table, nestle the creased paper pages inside the book. Use a pencil to mark three equally spaced holes on the inside crease. Now, on the cutting board to prevent tabletop dents, place the awl (or nail) on one of the marked areas, then tap it with the hammer until it creates a small hole. Gently wiggle the awl a bit to be sure the hole is open and is the correct size for the needle. Repeat these steps for the other two holes.

5. Thread the needle with embroidery floss; don't worry about knotting the floss. For sewing, follow the illustrated instructions:

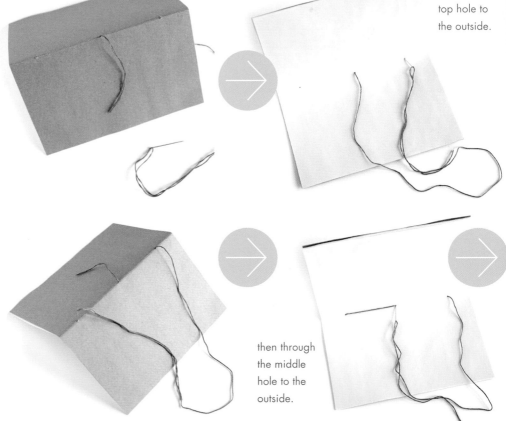

Beginning on the outside of the book, push the needle through the middle hole to the inside of the book . . .

Push the needle back through the bottom hole to the inside of the book . . .

then out the top hole to the outside.

then through the middle hole to the outside.

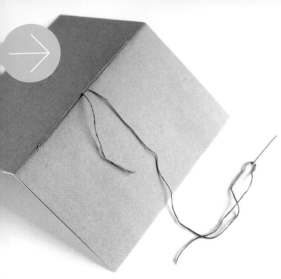

Both ends of the floss should be hanging on the outside of the book. Double-knot these loose ends and then trim them to about 1".

6. If desired, use the corner-rounding punch to put a nice curve on the corners of the cover and paper.

7. Now you have a blank book. It's time to think about decorating the cover and its contents!

MATERIALS

- collage materials
- craft glue
- pencil
- art marker

Collage Storybook

A collaged cover may be either realistic or abstract.

1. Use repurposed and found collage materials to create a cover design.

Magazines, catalogs, junk mail, old dictionaries, and scrap paper are perfect for this. Pay special attention to making the cover and title bold and captivating. For a shape collage, draw a shape with a black art marker, and then fill it in with collage materials.

2. Once the cover is finished, children will create a collaged picture for each page. Use one of the Story Starter games, such as Story Disks (page 23), Story Dice (page 32), or Story Grab Bag (page 40), to help children "write" their books. Older children might plan out which words and pictures will go on each page; younger children might be a bit more spontaneous. It all depends on their storytelling personality. It often helps to encourage younger children to create their pictures first and add words later, if they'd like to. Some children just learning to construct words may feel anxious about filling the pages with writing. Assure them that adding words is optional; they can make a picture book without words if that's most comfortable.

collage storybook

Memory Book

1. Ask children to brainstorm and think about a life moment they would like to share in their storybook. It might help to talk with parents, other family members, or friends who can contribute more details about the story. Perhaps a child wants to write about a hike up a mountain. Or maybe she will write about the first time she dived off the diving board or rode a horse by herself. She could even tell the story of a dream. The possibilities are rich and diverse.

2. Have children design engaging, colorful covers that reflect the story that will be told.

other neat ideas

>> This book would be a perfect Mother's Day, Father's Day, or sibling birthday gift. A child can make a book that compiles his favorite memories of a family member. Wouldn't that be a treasured gift!

>> Make a joint book with someone who shared an experience with you.

>> Write "My Story" on the cover of blank Storybooks, and give them to children in their party bags.

>> Make a book about a treasured family vacation. Read the story periodically throughout the year as a reminder.

>> Make a book about lessons learned and give to a teacher as an end-of-the-year gift.

memory book

HOW TO USE

This craft is particularly nice for groups of people who are just getting to know each other. After each person makes and assembles a book, he or she can write and illustrate or collage a story to share with the group. When used as an ice-breaker, having everyone tell a personal story with the same theme or from the same category is an effective way to inspire conversation. For example, ask the group to write funny stories, stories about their earliest memories, or stories about learning to do something that felt challenging. Another possibility is a story that illustrates a trait members of the group are proud of. The storybook can also serve as a personal journal where private ideas and artwork are created. There are so many possibilities.

HEY, ADULTS!

These books are certainly not just for kids. An adult might write a book about the time her oldest son tricked her into thinking the tour guide at Hershey Park told the line of onlookers that it's perfectly fine to step over the rope to pluck a Hershey's Kiss off the display pile. Or she might write her book about her neighborhood, dedicating each page to a different house/neighbor. Maybe she'd write about her adventure driving across the country, and she could highlight six or seven ministries from their trip. Or perhaps she would write about her favorite meals to cook for guests. She could dedicate each page to the details about the food and drink, as well as about the company she was feeding. This storytelling craft, in particular, is for people of all ages, from the earliest writers to the oldest thinkers.

Story City

These unique, colorful city buildings provide children with the chance to create new, imaginary worlds where fascinating stories unfold. Use recycled boxes and cartons from the kitchen to make a modern, playful city that can be rearranged and added to again and again.

TIME
To make: 2–3
hands-on hours

AGES
To make: 5+
(with adult help)

To use: 3+

PLAYERS
1+

MATERIALS
- scissors
- thick cardboard boxboard (from shipping boxes)
- paintbrushes and paints
- pencil
- ruler
- cardstock in a variety of colors
- craft glue
- toothpicks
- small round wooden beads (with toothpick-size holes)
- vitamin bottles filled with sand (optional)
- small rocks (optional)

Once you learn the crafting technique, you'll be able to make shops, skyscrapers, apartment buildings — or make up your own types of buildings. The variations are endless. A shop, for example, could be a delicatessen, a barber shop, a grocery, or a pharmacy. I like bright, playful colors for the buildings, and I often make the roofs a contrasting color.

HOW TO MAKE
The Skyscraper

1. Cut a 7" × 4" rectangle with a triangular top out of the thick boxboard. You may also want to skip the triangle point and simply have a rectangular skyscraper. Paint it with two different bright colors (one for the triangular top and one for the rectangular bottom).

2. While the building is drying, make the windows by measuring, drawing, and cutting eight equal-size 1" squares out of cardstock. To make the door, cut a 1½" × 2" rectangle out of a different-color cardstock. Once the building is fully dry, glue the windows and door onto its face.

3. To make a small antenna for the tippy-top point of the skyscraper, glue a painted toothpick to the back of the apex of the triangle. Attach a small wooden bead to the top of the toothpick with a bit of glue. Set aside to dry.

The Shop

1. Cut a 6" × 7½" rectangle out of the thick boxboard. Paint the building with two different bright colors (one for the square bottom and one for the thin rectangular top).

2. While the paint is drying, cut a 2" × 3" door and two 2" square windows out of cardstock. Decide what kind of store it is, then make a little sign for it. For example, for a tailor's shop, make a little picture of a needle and thread to hang on the front. Once the shop is fully dry, glue the windows and door onto the face of the building.

The Apartment Building

1. Cut an 8" × 5" rectangle out of the thick boxboard. Paint the rectangle with any bright color you like.

2. While the building is drying, make the windows and door. For the windows, cut twelve 1" squares out of cardstock; make a door by cutting a 1½" × 2" rectangle out of a different-color cardstock. Once the apartment is fully dry, glue the windows (four rows of three) and door onto the face of the building.

All Buildings

Use these instructions to make a variety of buildings, such as a police station, a flower shop, and a grocery store. In order to make buildings stable and upright, use a heavy-duty craft glue to attach vitamin containers filled with sand to the backs of the buildings. This will enable them to stand tall and protects them from being easily knocked over. If you prefer to use a more rugged option, small rocks will work well, too.

Cut rectangle out of thick boxboard. Paint the building and roof each a different color.

Cut square "windows" out of cardstock.

Use heavy-duty craft glue to attach vitamin containers filled with sand to the backs of buildings.

HOW TO USE

Children can rearrange the buildings until they've made the city of their dreams. Encourage them to have little people (Story Stones, for example, page 57) make their way through the imaginary metropolis. Invite them to create different stories about the people who live and work in the buildings. They can give them names and decide where they live, what they do, and what their lives are like. Imagine the different businesses and people who work inside the skyscraper: doctors, scientists, architects, builders, and bankers.

other neat ideas

» Use buildings to make a miniature version of your neighborhood. Make apartments or houses as appropriate.

» Make a magical village with shops that sell rainbows and businesses that translate secret codes.

» Make mushrooms with doors and windows for a fairy or gnome village.

TEACHING TIP

If your cardboard has bold lettering or symbols, coat it first with a layer of white paint (as a cover-up), then paint it with bright colors.

The Briney Sea

fairy village

the tippy top Mountain range

tin city

the troubled forest

Goose egg farm

Lucky's clover patch

Sunshine field

The Grassy Knoll

the rambling river

Sunfish Wharf

blueberry island

Cuffy's campground

Pebble beach

lavender fields

Flax Cove

Craggy beach

Tangerine bridge

Popcorn village

Muggy marsh

minnow island

Sunfish Bay

Story Map

Children can use this Story Map to create stories about an
imaginary place. Set it on the ground so that small figurines can
dance across the land. Roll it neatly and reuse it again and again
to initiate storytelling. Specific details, such as dungeons and
pirate ships and farms, can be added to the map as they come to
life in a story.

TIME
To make: **2–3 hours**

AGES
To make: **5+**

To use: **5+**

PLAYERS
1+

HOW TO MAKE

1. Make a list of all of the unique features of the imaginary land. Does it
   have water? Hills? Islands? Deserts?
   Encourage the children's creativity;

the hills can be purple and the mud
pits can be made of chocolate. The
more fantastical and far-reaching the
details, the more useful they will be
for storytelling.

➤ notepaper
➤ pencils
➤ scissors
➤ newsprint
➤ thin black art marker
➤ colored pencils
➤ watercolors
➤ old travel magazines or old maps (optional)

Use pictures from old travel magazines and/or old maps to guide the children, or they can collage pictures to add depth and creativity to their map.

2. Once the list is substantial enough, cut a piece of newsprint to size, then ask children to draw, with the #2 pencils, the outline of their land, including the outline of all of the detailed features. Older crafters can refer to their list on their own, but younger crafters will need an adult to remind them of their land's physical and geological features. Don't get too hung up on the scale and size of details; they aren't nearly as important as the imaginative qualities they bring to the map.

3. Use art markers and colored pencils to add color to small details, such as trees, water, hills, a farm, a castle, cities, roads, bridges, and flower fields.

4. Have children use watercolors to fill in the remainder of their design (water, grass, and so forth).

5. With a black art marker, trace around the perimeter of the land. This will give the map's boundaries added definition. At this time, children can use the black marker to give the roads, forests, parks, and buildings original names. They can also write important side notes giving further explanations about specific parts of the map.

other neat ideas

➤➤ Make a treasure map to use in a dramatic story adventure.

➤➤ Make a map of a familiar place (your neighborhood, school, or vacation spot).

➤➤ Create a Story Map of your brain, heart, or stomach in which you depict things you often think about, love, or love to eat.

TEACHING TIP
Read a story aloud, then ask your students to create a Story Map based on its details. Be sure to select a story that lends itself to mapmaking.

Story Soundtrack

This writing adventure makes children think about the emotional atmosphere of a story and gives them practice matching the tone and emotion of different parts of a story with a variety of songs. This activity is best with just one child, as it involves listening to multiple individual choices.

TIME
To make: **2–3 hours**

AGES
5+

PLAYERS
1+

MATERIALS
- copy of a story (preferably one that your child has written)
- pen or pencil
- instrument (optional)
- some sort of music player
- a wide selection of songs
- a computer program that makes playlists (optional)

HOW TO DO IT

1. Read the chosen story aloud and spend a bit of time discussing character, setting, mood, and tone. The story shouldn't be too long — just long enough to have a variety of emotions, plot points, and perhaps settings. Talk about the words and images that make something gloomy, happy, scary, or surprising. Discuss what kind of music would pair well with each mood, and take note of it in the story's margins.

2. Use an instrument to create music, or listen to different tunes to find the best musical fit. An adult should help with the music technicalities, such as making the stereo work and stopping and moving on if a song isn't right. Adults can also suggest songs or artists. As the child finds songs that fit perfectly, be sure to have him write the song in the margin next to the specific section of the story.

3. Once the child is satisfied with his song list, go through the story and spend time coordinating where the songs should begin and end. Keep in mind that it might be difficult to play songs with words while a story is being told. In this case, the story can briefly pause as the song (or a portion of it) plays, and then the story can continue. If you have access to a computer music program (such as iTunes or Windows Media Player), create a digital playlist. If not, line up your song selections in the order they need to play. Invite friends and family to gather for a musical story time, and play the soundtrack or instrument while you or your child reads aloud.

other **neat** ideas

>> Give the Story Soundtrack as a gift.

>> Play and listen to a song that has a story in it, then have children retell the story in their own words.

>> Have kids dramatically act out the story while the music plays.

>> With musically inclined children, record them making their own music to go with their stories.

Storytelling Kit

Use any combination of projects from these first two chapters to create imaginative, action-packed traveling Storytelling Kits. Create your own unique combination with your child. These kits are perfect for creative play in the car, an airplane, a hotel, or a friend's house.

TIME
To make: **2 hours**

AGES
To make: **5+**

To use: **5+**

PLAYERS
1+

HOW TO MAKE

1. Decide what you want your Storytelling Kit to include, choosing from any of the projects in the book.

Here are some ideas:

➤ Story Mat (page 66), 8 Story Stones (page 57), and some Story Sparks (page 50)

➤ 3 Story Stones (page 57), a set of Story Disks (page 23), a mini Collage Storybook (page 74), and some Story Sparks (page 50)

➤ Traveling Puppet Theater (page 60), Story-Disk Chain (page 94), and 3 Story Stones

➤ Storybook (page 72), Story Dice (page 32), 4 Story Stones, and 8 Story Disks (page 23)

➤ Story Grab Bag (page 40), Storybook, 8 Story Disks, and some Story Sparks

2. Package the Storytelling Kit in a small muslin bag, a shoebox, a small travel bag, or even a small brown-paper grocery bag. Just be sure to have some sort of container so your children will be able to keep track of the small pieces.

TEACHING TIP

Have each child make a personalized, unique Storytelling Kit. When it's time for creative writing or creative storytelling, children can quietly use the kits at their desks to make up new stories. This is a great way to foster individuality and independence within the classroom.

rocket
ship

flying
saucer

meteor
trails

. . . just then, a flying saucer came out of nowhere . . .

3 story activities

fun practice in creative word use, group storytelling, and narrative thinking

It's not what you look at that matters, it's what you see.

— HENRY DAVID THOREAU

With some thought and purpose, a walk down a city street can be transformed. The zooming taxi might be transporting two children who have just arrived from Istanbul and are now rushing to a fancy ball. Maybe the person at the hotdog stand is really a wizard, and perhaps the pigeons in the park have stories of their own to tell. A hotdog vendor is almost always a hotdog vendor, but with some purposeful thinking, we can use our powerful, imaginative minds to think differently. With clever, thoughtful interpretations, a walk in the woods, a trip to the petting farm, a night at a street fair, or a visit to a shop can be a surprising source of storytelling inspiration.

Children often find themselves instinctively engaged in this kind of imaginative thinking. The Story Activities in this chapter will help direct and encourage them to think like storytellers.

→ Maybe the person at the hotdog stand is really a wizard.

These activities focus on the *process*, not just the product. Together, you and the children will move, search, think, remember, guess, and play your way to a bounty of vivid stories. When children are asked to draw or write about their stories, ideas, and experiences, encourage them to enjoy drawing and not think about the finished product. A child who discovers that her boat doesn't look like the boat she imagined in her story might feel discouraged. Remind the children that whatever they write or draw is unique to them and their specific story, and that's what makes it special. Help them celebrate the inspired stories and ideas that come forth.

PUT ON YOUR STORY GOGGLES

To participate in the activities in this chapter, ask your children to put on their "story goggles." Tell them that with these goggles on, their eyes will see regular things a little differently. The goggles will help them notice curious, unique objects; interesting people and animals; and clever conversation. The ability to shift from regularly observing the world to searching for inspiration is a crucial step in the creative process. It means children are beginning to understand that they can *choose* to think creatively when they want to and that their unique interpretations of their surroundings are useful, wonderful things. Recognizing this is empowering and liberating. With books and pencils in hand and their story goggles on, they will be in charge of their creative worlds.

Storytelling Walk

This is an outdoor adventure during which children mentally collect five objects each, so be sure they are ready with notebook in hand. When they return, they draw and paint the objects and then use all five to tell their stories.

TIME
4 hours (multiple steps and stages; over a few days is ideal)

AGES
3+ (with modifications for the youngest child)

PLAYERS
2+

MATERIALS
- a notebook
- pencils
- small pencil sharpener
- colored pencils
- pail or small bucket
- waterproof art markers
- watercolors
- watercolor paper
- paintbrushes
- hole punch
- twine or embroidery floss

HOW TO DO IT

1. Decide where to go. Although a walk in a park or in the woods is inspiring and fruitful, don't limit yourself to a nature walk. You can also explore city or town streets, an outdoor flea market, a petting farm, or a school.

2. Before setting forth, ask your children to put on their "story goggles" and encourage them to walk and observe with purpose. This teaches them to switch to creative-thinking mode. Bring a notebook for recording, a small set of colored pencils, and pencils for each child. Bring along a small pencil sharpener, just in case.

3. During the walk, each child mentally collects five items; these will become the foundation for a story. Once a child decides that an item is worth collecting, she writes a short description along with a sketch of the item in her notebook.

   Encourage children to use colored pencils to make their depictions as accurate as possible. Some items, such as small pebbles and seedpods that have fallen on the ground, may be collected in a pail and brought home. (To be environmentally sensitive, please do not allow groups of children to pick flowers and leaves from bushes and trees.)

other neat things

>> Do a Storytelling Walk for every season. Once a full year of walks is completed, bind the four stories to make one seasonal storytelling book.

>> For some challenging fun, make it a guessing game. Have a child read her story aloud, then ask the other children to guess which objects within the story were the original five found items.

4. Once each child has "collected" five items, return home or to the classroom. Have children spend time looking at their descriptions and sketches. Give each child a waterproof art marker, a set of watercolors, some sheets of water-color paper, and paintbrushes. Ask children to use the art marker to draw a picture of each of their items. Once the marker is dry, children will use watercolors to give the items depth. This technique is nice because it allows the lines of the drawings to remain visible even after the translucent color is applied.

5. As the paintings dry, ask the children to begin writing or telling a story that contains all five collected items. Depending on their ages, this part of the activity can take ten minutes to a few hours. The youngest child can simply talk about and describe each object, then ask her to tell you a little story about each one. Parents and teachers can model the storytelling process by telling their own short story, incorporating five of the children's objects.

6. Bind each final written story with the five pictures to create a story-book. Do this with a hole punch and twine or embroidery floss (see Storybook, page 72). If you've done this project with a group of children, offer them the chance to tell their stories to the group. If not, the child might want to show and tell his story to family and friends.

Simple memories from the walk translated into watercolors.

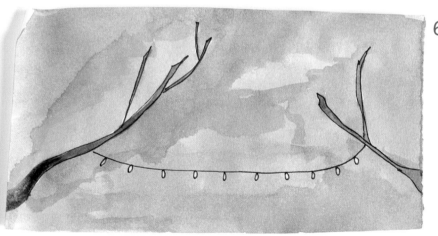

→ **TEACHING TIP**
Teachers can bring their class on a Storytelling Walk field trip. Spend half the time in the field and the rest of the time creating their stories.

Picture Tales

This activity asks kids to consider how a visual snapshot fits into the broader context of a story, and then gives them practice in writing in a stream-of-consciousness style.

TIME
1 hour

AGES
6+

PLAYERS
2+

MATERIALS
- dilapidated picture books or photography books
- old art-history textbooks
- record album covers
- art and nature magazines
- paper and pencil

TEACHING TIP
Keep a basket full of these pictures available to use as creative writing prompts.

HOW TO PLAY

1. Gather an eclectic assortment of pictures from a variety of sources. For this game, it's best if the pictures depict a scene, a person doing something, or a grouping of objects or people. Bring your pictures to the copy shop to have them laminated; that way, they'll last for years.

2. Have children clear their minds before beginning, and explain that this is a chance to write without thinking about *how* or *why*. Show one picture at a time to the children, then encourage them to write everything and anything that comes into their minds. Tell them not to worry about grammar, spelling, or sentence structure. Describe the ideas as flowing through their minds and landing directly on their paper.

3. After they have written their own word associations about a picture, ask a few directed questions: some general, others tailored to the specific image. This will encourage them to delve deeper into the fictional story. Here are some general questions:

   - Where is the picture taken and who lives there?

   - What was happening just before the photograph was taken? Just after?

   - Who took the picture and why?

4. Afterward, children can compare ideas and stories. They may also use details and story frames from their Picture Tales to create lengthier, more elaborate stories.

other neat things

>> Use old family pictures taken before a child was born.

>> Play detective! Give children five pictures and tell them they're all connected, then ask them to write a tale that tells how and why.

>> Have a group of children draw their own pictures. Randomly redistribute these pictures, and ask each child to tell a tale about the one she received.

Truth or Tale?

This lively group game gives children the opportunity to practice telling true and false stories in an effort to make them as realistic and believable as possible. In deciphering whether a story is a truth or a tale, they have to think about what details and structures make stories plausible and convincing. It also asks them to listen to others' stories with a discerning ear, so they can begin to judge when they're willing to believe in the stories others tell. This is not just an exercise in determining what is real and what is made up, but also a practice in deciding how to build a convincing, compelling tale — whether or not it is true.

HOW TO DO IT

TIME
1 hour

AGES
5+

PLAYERS
2+ (more is better!)

MATERIALS
➤ paper and pencil

1. The game is best played with people who aren't intimately familiar with all of the details of your life history. Begin by asking the players to draw two columns on their paper — one labeled TRUTH and the other TALE. Then, in the appropriate columns, have them write three brief summaries of true stories from their lives and three brief summaries of false events. Encourage them to note specific details and to keep them private. Before beginning the game, have players find a quiet corner to softly practice telling their stories aloud.

2. The first player chooses one of his stories to tell aloud to the group. He should tell it as convincingly as possible with vivid details. When he is finished, the rest of the players (the audience) take turns saying whether they thought it was a truth or a tale, with reasons to back up their decision. Ideally, the group forms a consensus, then the storyteller discloses which kind it was. Players can engage in a discussion about the reasons for their conclusion. The audience and the first player then talk about what storytelling strategies worked and which didn't. When the discussion period is over, it is the next player's turn to tell a story. Encourage the children to use what they learned in the first round to inform their second round of stories. The game ends when each player has had a chance to tell one story. Play another round if you'd like.

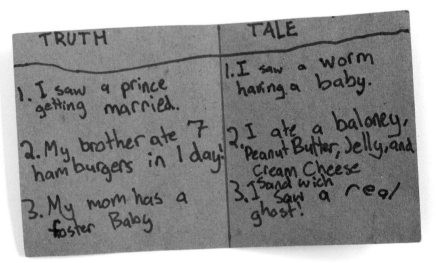

TRUTH

1. I saw a prince getting married.

2. My brother ate 7 hamburgers in 1 day!

3. My mom has a foster Baby

TALE

1. I saw a worm having a baby.

2. I ate a baloney, Peanut Butter, Jelly, and Cream Cheese Sandwich

3. I saw a real ghost!

Use this as a fun way to practice public speaking.

TRUTH

1. I saw a prince getting married.

2. My brother ate 7 hamburgers in 1 day!

3. My mom has a foster Baby

TALE

1. I saw _

2. I at Peanu[t] _

3. _

other **neat** things

>> Play Truth or Tale? at a birthday party.

>> Use the game as an icebreaker for a group of children who are just getting to know each other. It's team building and fun, and kids will learn a little bit about their new friends.

Fill In the Blanks

This activity provides simple, creative, and often silly fun. In the face of a story frame with missing words, kids fill in the blanks in the most creative way possible. This is similar to Mad Libs, but children are aware of the story's context as they fill in the missing words. Fill In the Blanks is best played in a group so that there is a wide variety of suggestions.

HOW TO DO IT

TIME
1 hour

AGES
3+

PLAYERS
2+

MATERIALS
➤ paper and pen

1. In preparation for the game, an adult or older child writes the story frame, leaving out important details, characters, and descriptions, with just a line where the word(s) should be. It is helpful to include enough story lines and solid leads that your child can easily plug in missing words.

An example of a brief story frame (frames can be much more elaborate):

Sasha woke up early and decided to go on an adventure to search for _____.

She dressed in a _____ shirt and _____ pants. After she ate some _____,

she was on her way. At the beginning of her journey, she came upon (a/n)

_____ who made a big _____, which left her feeling _____.

She was curious to find out what was on the other side of the bend, so she continued

on. Shortly after walking through a field of _____, she was so surprised to

see (a/n) _____. She said, "_____" and then tossed _____ in her

backpack. When she arrived at _____, she ate a picnic lunch of _____

and then climbed on a _____ for fun. As the sun was getting low, she was

thrilled to finally discover _____, which looked like (a/n) _____, felt like

(a/n) _____, and smelled like (a/n) _____. She decided to bring it

_____. As she walked back to her warm house, she thought about what a

_____ day it had been.

2. Read the story frame, and then ask your child to creatively fill in the blanks as the story progresses. Encourage him to take his time choosing words, and remind him to think beyond the most obvious choices. A child as young as three years old can enjoy the game, but he might need a bit more guidance and explanation as he fills in the blanks.

A family of FAIRIES were preparing for a celebration dinner at the BALL ROOM. They had waited all year to celebrate THE HARVEST so it was bound to be a spectacular event filled with FOOD and FUN GAMES. The middle child in the family, named SPARKLE, was busy with final preparations. S/he had been given the special job of making sure the ROOM didn't get MESSY or DISTURBED. It took up lots of (her) time, but s/he was glad s/he had worked hard on it. A wise aunt was in charge of the menu, and she decided that the food would all be FANCY PIES and decorated with STARS. How EXCITING! When it was time to get dressed for the night, they all put on their best FLOWER PETALS which all had the same BOWS. As the happy guests arrived, there was dancing and CORNETS and PICKING FOOD. It was a night to remember! And, a GIANT PUMPKIN to remember too!

Here's a finished story after I played with Leah, age 6.

When the story blanks are all filled in, read the improvised story aloud, and then ask your child if he would like to fill in the blanks again! He'll be delighted at the many different stories that come from the same story frame.

3. If you are playing with a group of children, read the story frame aloud, then they take turns filling in the blanks or have them each fill in the blanks on his or her own separate piece of paper. Read the completed stories together. If children all did their own stories, you can have a lively discussion about similarities and differences.

TEACHING TIP Create a variety of blank stories, and have children use them in pairs or partners as a way to practice creative writing and vocabulary. Also, in a kind of reverse of the Fill In the Blanks game, ask students to write a story frame for a preexisting vocabulary list. Then, as a way to practice that vocabulary, children can swap stories and fill in each other's using the vocabulary words.

And here is the drawing she made to go with the story.

other neat ideas

>> Make a book of Fill In the Blanks stories and use them as quiet activities before bedtime, on long car rides, or at a birthday party.

>> Have children draw a picture to go along with their new story.

>> After crossing out a few words on every page of a very worn storybook, have children fill in the blanks. It's great fun to see how the story changes.

Story-Disk Chain

The Story-Disk Chain provides children with practice in ordering and structuring stories and, at the same time, encourages them to retell a story. This retelling is how stories become internalized, and it's exciting and rewarding to watch your child learn to tell a story that's true to the order on the story chain.

TIME
To make: **1–2 hands-on hours**

AGES
To make: **5+ (with an adult)**

To use: **3+**

PLAYERS
1+

MATERIALS
➤ **pencil**
➤ **stencil for a circle 2" in diameter (or a vitamin container or jam-jar lid)**
➤ **cereal-box panels**
➤ **scissors**
➤ **craft paint and brushes**
➤ **wax paper**
➤ **thin black art marker**
➤ **heavy book**
➤ **hole punch**
➤ **thin cord**

HOW TO MAKE

1. Decide how many disks you want to make for your story. I usually try for eight. With a pencil and the circle stencil, trace circles onto the cereal-box panels and then carefully cut them out. Paint the disks in a variety of playful, cheery colors. Paint one side first, let dry on some wax paper, then paint the other side (after the first side has fully dried). Continue to do this until all the disks are evenly coated with paint.

2. Once the disks are fully dry, have children use the black art marker to draw images of people, places, things, animals, emotions, or numbers onto them. Encourage children to keep each drawing as simple as possible. Because the disks have a tendency to curl after they're painted, put a heavy book over them overnight to flatten them.

3. Use the hole punch to make two holes on opposite sides of each disk. This step tends to be fun for the over-three set.

4. Sort disks and create a group that works nicely together to tell a story. Use the cord to tie a knot on the first disk. (Take care not to tie it too tight; that could tear the disk. In addition, loose knots mean that you can easily rearrange the disks in order to tell new stories.) Find the next in line and tie the cord to it. Continue doing this until the story chain is complete.

HOW TO USE

1. Hang the chain vertically in a play space, classroom, or child's bedroom for an instant storytelling reminder. Tuck it in a backpack or travel bag, so she can tell her story to friends and family.

2. Have children use the Story-Disk Chain to practice memorizing stories. Choose a story chain that a child hasn't looked at in a long time, and have him hold the chain while telling a story according to the specific order on the chain. Ask him to tell the same story one more time while looking at the chain. Then, take away the chain and see if he can remember the correct order of events. Of course, show him the chain if he stumbles and see if he wants to try again. This process of envisioning each part, each vivid image, of the story is good practice for young storytellers.

other neat ideas

>> Punch the holes closer to the top of the disks, and use the chain as a garland. String across the doorway for festive cheer; it will liven up the room and get people thinking.

>> Make themed chains: silly, kind, mysterious, wacky.

>> Make a "perfect day" chain in which the chain documents, in order, everything that would happen on an idyllic day.

Build a Story

This is a versatile group-storytelling game in which each person collects items and incorporates one of them into a large, collaborative story. Because it uses very few materials, it can be played anywhere and in short bursts of time.

TIME
1–2 hours

AGES
5+ (plus an older child or an adult)

PLAYERS
3+

MATERIALS
➤ bucket or sack for collecting
➤ paper and pencil

HOW TO DO IT

1. The group disperses (outside or inside) on a hunt for interesting objects. Collectors should scan their surroundings for unique, amusing, mysterious, curious, or even mundane objects and put the best ones in their buckets. An item might be a stone, branch, little shovel, spoon, handkerchief, flower, hammer, map, watch, or teacup. Once the buckets are filled, each person should spend time alone sifting through his findings in order to choose one item to bring to the group story. Sometimes the most ordinary objects can add a fascinating dimension to a tale, so encourage storytellers to simply choose the object that feels right.

2. To begin the group narrative, the children should be sitting in a circle with their chosen object in front

Small flea market finds or natural elements can be inspiration for big stories.

of them. The first person begins the story by setting the scene and including her object. The next person creates a transition into his part of the narrative and then does his best to smoothly and imaginatively incorporate his object. The game continues this way until the last one or two people use their objects to end the story.

other **neat** ideas

>> Play Build a Story at a birthday party or use it as a "get-to-know-you" game.

>> Have kids draw a picture of one scene of the completed story.

>> Add another dimension to the game by asking someone from outside the group to add an object at any point during the game. Have the children make a group decision as to how it should be incorporated.

3. As the story is told, someone outside the group should record it as completely as possible. If time allows, participants can trade their objects for different ones from their buckets and the group can tell a whole new story.

Word Tags

Words make us think. They are small kernels of meaning that inspire and surprise. Become word collectors and use your bounty to write vibrant poems and tell interesting stories. As children explore and play with words, they learn to love using language in unique, new ways. Make piles of these words to encourage fun, imaginative wordplay.

TIME
To make: **1 hour**

AGES
6+

PLAYERS
1+

MATERIALS
➤ cardstock
➤ scissors
➤ art marker
➤ tape
➤ paper

HOW TO MAKE

To make the tags, cut 2" × 1½" rectangles out of various colors of cardstock. Don't pay too much attention to cutting perfect right angles; most of our Word Tags are crooked and lopsided, which I find endearing. Make lots of tags, and once you have an abundance, write one word on each tag with a contrasting-color marker. Open your mind and invite words to come. Don't worry about spelling or choosing words from certain categories. If a word is compelling or interesting or unique, add it to your collection. Carry a notepad with you for times when an alluring word pops into your head when you are away from home.

A sample Word Tag collection:

- loop
- lavender
- persnickety
- gray
- Poseidon
- hidden
- clamor
- tussle
- tangerine
- wizard
- creek
- slope
- clasp
- woodchuck
- stalagmite
- smashup
- bookish
- wilt
- flub
- avalanche
- nubbin
- grip
- woolly
- blush
- mud
- dream
- marigold
- brine
- aloft
- junket
- outfox
- bedrock
- fly

- zero
- twirl
- curve
- dragon
- crackerjack
- sneer
- pie
- maze
- whimsy
- pebbles
- smooth
- clatter
- weepy
- clunk
- sassafrass
- tang
- lost
- feather
- chick
- rooted
- canopy
- hoot
- sidewise
- howl
- gnome
- aqua
- wee
- roses
- maudlin
- tuft
- robot
- goof
- milkweed

HOW TO USE

1. Store Word Tags in jars and bowls in places where children can easily reach them.

2. Tape Word Tags to different objects around the house. Maybe a book spine has the word *ambassador* on it or a basket of apples has the words *buggy barrels* on it.

3. Use bits of tape and tags to create poems on paper, inside cabinets, and on bedroom doors.

4. Make a word soup by swishing the words together in the center of a table, then go fishing for words.

5. Make impromptu poems, trade them, make sentences, choose your favorite word of the day, arrange, and rearrange. When using the tags for poem building, encourage your children to use small words (*the, to, in, a*) to link the Word Tag words.

trumpet king
a feast
a rose of stars
lost in the flower forest
tunnel to the castle stairs
listen to the mystery bells
creep home

6. Practice combining random words to create imaginary words:

   - cold kiss
   - orbit coil
   - tear split
   - jet bug
   - rose peel
   - paper lane

7. Immerse yourselves in words and play with them freely.

other **neat** ideas

>> Create a family ritual in which each day you choose a word from your Word Tag collection and use it in an interesting way.

>> Use Word Tags as a game at a birthday party. Have each child choose ten words and then make a short poem with them. Read the poems aloud.

>> Have children draw tiny pictures on the other side of the Word Tags.

Word Lists

Similar to Word Tags, Word Lists give children a chance to explore and enjoy word manipulation. This activity is a bit more channeled and focused, though, as it asks children to consider how words relate to each other. It's good practice at brainstorming for creative ideas while telling or writing stories. The beauty of this activity is that each person will have an original, clever, inspired list.

TIME
1 hour

AGES
7+

PLAYERS
1+

MATERIALS
➤ paper and pencils

HOW TO DO IT

Create a variety of list prompts and ask children to answer the prompt in list form. Ask them to stick to the list's prompt, and encourage them to continue searching for ideas even if they feel like they've thought of everything. Often, the best ideas come to us when we think we're done; the extra bit of mental probing can produce magnificent ideas.

♡I♡Love...♡

1 ★ Green
2 ★ Dogs
3 ★ Dance (IRISH STEP)
4 ★ Rock Climbing
5 ★ Cows
6 ★ MoM + Dad
7 ★ Writing
8 ★ Poetry
9 ★ grapes
10 ★ Apple Juce
11 ★ Softball
12 ★ field hocky
13 ★ Cookies
14 ★ Stuft animals
15 ★ Rain
16 ★ family
17 ★ friends
18 ★ Movies
19 ★ Owls
20 ★ Clarenet!
21 ★ Alto Saxiphone's

What I love:

1. awesome stuff
2. PUPPY'S
3. kit kat candy
4. my mom
5. my dad
d. my brother
7. me ♡
8 HHHmmm...
9. my grandma
lo. my toys
ll. my stuffed peinguine pinpin
12. my family
13. HHHMMM...

other neat ideas

>> Make imaginary shopping lists.

>> Make a list for every color in the rainbow (and more).

>> Create a story character and make a list for him based on his personality.

Examples of prompts:

I love . . .

In 10 years I'll see . . .

My name is . . .

Blue is for . . .

A bird knows . . .

When I lie in the grass . . .

The ground knows . . .

I was born to . . .

When I look at the sky, I see . . .

Snow makes me feel . . .

Example: The ocean is . . .

briny and deep

crashing

rippling

building waves

tossing boats

aqua

secret island

ship sailing home

messages in bottles

empty ships under the sea

seashells and rounded glass

gulls crying

Example: Green is . . .

tomatillos

garden tea

shag carpet

Key lime pie

scaly monster skin

flat, warm grass

pine trees

a fresh, warm morning

happy eyes

meadow paths

Jell-O

bouncy balls

Blue makes me think of

Sonic the hedghog
Mario
luigi
tails
Knukles
Sky
Pie
Sea
Popcorn
dogs
Toad

Shell spiral, turreted; spire often acute; epidermis dark, thick; operculum notched or chambered in front; outer lip sharp; operculum horny, spiral.

Animal with broad, short, foot; broad, non-retractile snout; tentacles far apart, bearing short eyestalks; tongue long, slim, with seven series of many-cusped teeth; mantle margin fringed; gill of stiff, cylindrical plates. Reproduction often viviparous.

A large family inhabiting fresh water lakes and rivers, in warm regions, chiefly of the Old World.

Genus MELANIA, Lam.

Shell with acute apex, its whorls ornamented with spines or striations; aperture oval, pointed above. Four hundred species, distributed over Southern Europe, India, Philippines, Pacific Islands, in swift tidal rivers, especially in rapids.

The Melanias include forms with cancellated, tubercled and smooth shells. They range from globose to needle-like forms. The largest is under three inches long. Many species have their shells decollated — broken off at the apex. The finest species are Philippine.

The **Acorn Black Snail** (*M. glans, Busch*) is smooth, oval, olive-hued, with a depressed spire; the body whorl and the aperture are large. Length, 1 inch.

Habitat, Philippines.

The **F**ij**k Snail** (*M. setosa, Swains.*) is globose and has its sp.. a spiral row of erect sharp spines. The black or gree.. ntrasts with the pale lip and throat. Length, 1½ inc...

...lippines, Fiji Islands.

...Lea, is fawn-coloured and long and tapering

184

The Reference Desk

In this interesting game, a group of children use various reference and information books as story generators. Each person takes a turn blindly choosing a word from one of the books and then incorporating that word into the group story. The only control a player has over the word choice is deciding which book it will come from.

HOW TO PLAY

TIME
1 hour

AGES
7+

PLAYERS
3+

REFERENCE MATERIALS
➤ phonebook (for names)
➤ encyclopedia
➤ textbooks (biology, history, earth science)
➤ atlas
➤ thesaurus
➤ bird guide
➤ tree guide
➤ insect guide

1. A group of people sit in a circle with a pile of various reference books in the center. The first person chooses one of the books, opens it up to a random page, closes his eyes, points his finger somewhere on the page, opens his eyes, and sees where his finger has landed. For example, if a child uses a phonebook, he incorporates in his story whatever name his finger lands on.

2. Once he has gone as far as he sees fit, the next player does the same thing and continues the story. This goes on until all players have had at least one turn or until there is group consensus that the story is complete.

TEACHING TIPS

Librarians and teachers can use the Reference Desk game to help children become familiar with the different kinds of reference books available to them:

> Use this as a language-building game. Use the words from the story as a student-generated vocabulary list.

> Foreign-language teachers can have students use just a foreign-language dictionary as they play. These words, too, can be a student-generated vocabulary list.

Create the Past

Everyone, every item — from the littlest piece of dirt to a giant skyscraper — has a story, a history behind it. This activity encourages kids to consider and create the context and backstory of all that surrounds us. It's the chance to give a full life to objects.

TIME
1 hour

AGES
5+

PLAYERS
1+

MATERIALS
- paper and pens
- various random objects

HOW TO DO IT

1. Explain to your children that everything has a history. Spend time talking about the fictional history of something, so they begin to see how in-depth, interesting, and creative a made-up story can be.

Here is a brief example of a fictional history of a piece of green beach glass. It could have many more details and plot lines, but its brevity works to demonstrate how to think backward into the previous life of an object.

It began as a handful of sand that floated in the water or rested on a sand dune, depending on the tide. One day a truck pulled close to some dunes, and a worker with a shovel began shoveling piles of sand into the back of the truck. The sand was brought to a factory, where it was cleaned, sorted, heated, and made into a green bowl. It was shipped to a department store and sat on a shelf there for eight months until a newly married couple bought it. The couple brought it home and it lived in the cabinet. Someone ate breakfeast out of it almost every morning. They fed both of their children from it, and when they died, it was sold at a yard sale to a college student. She used it to store rubber bands and bread clips, and when she moved to Florida, she brought it with her. She filled it with gravel, dirt, and some plants and set it on her balcony.

One day a gust of wind blew it off the balcony, and it broke into many pieces in the parking lot. One tiny piece blew into a marshy field. It stayed there for years, until a hurricane came to shore and the waves washed over the field. The piece of glass was dragged into the ocean, where it turned and turned in the waves until it was smooth and round. One morning, an older, retired couple were out for their daily beach walk when they happened upon the perfectly rounded piece of beach glass. It now hangs in their kitchen window, reminding them to pay attention to the beauty of their surroundings.

2. Display a collection of random items, both natural and synthetic. Ask the children to choose one item and to write down the story of its past. Describe its earliest beginnings. Was it made in a factory? If so, what did the factory look like? Describe the worker who made it. Was it owned? Who owned it? How was it used? Did all of its owners use it similarly?

Was it loved? Despised? Neglected? Was it well cared for or barely noticed?

Encourage children to give life, and perhaps even human characteristics, to the object. For example, how did the lone leaf feel when the autumn wind blew it off its branch? Free? Lonely? Excited to join the others?

TEACHING TIP
Make this a multi-disciplinary lesson in which children practice history, science, language arts, and creative arts. Ask the children to consider the time period and the science, as well as the creative story behind the object.

other neat ideas

>> Play Create the Past as a group and have all of the children write a historical story about the same object. Spend time comparing the unique stories.

>> Write the true story of a favorite personal object.

>> Write the history of an object from the viewpoint of the object. For example, an apron might begin her story, "I started life on a cotton plantation in Georgia."

Story Ping-Pong

This is one of the most casual, simple, and appealing games ever. Players pass a story back and forth until they're all happy with the ending. In doing so, the storytellers create a nice, comfortable rhythm and an engaging, collaborative tale. Each player must relinquish control over the storytelling process, which makes the game fun and carefree. With barely any rules or structure, the game is easy to take up at any given moment, and it can be played on and off whenever it strikes a group's fancy.

TIME
1 hour

AGES
5+

PLAYERS
3+

MATERIALS
➤ paper and pen
➤ small item for passing around (a Ping-Pong ball, pebble, or glove, for example)

It also happens to be one of my older daughter's favorites. She has been known to come into the bathroom while I'm showering, asking to play Story Ping-Pong with me. Some of my fondest memories of our collaborative storytelling involve steam, shampoo, and the sound of rushing water. This is what makes the game so valuable: It can make an ordinary time feel like an adventure. Plus, we end up laughing a lot whenever we play.

HOW TO DO IT

1. One player holds the ball and tells the opening portion of the story. When he is ready, he passes it on to another child.

2. The next person continues the story until she feels it is time to pass the ball to another player. This goes on until all players feel that the story is sufficiently complete. Of course, players can return to the story at any time in the future to add more to the ending. A player can hold on to the story for two minutes or two seconds; it's completely at the discretion of the storyteller.

3. It is important that each player respect one another's turn, allowing the story to go in whatever direction the storyteller leads it. When playing with young children, remind them to add as many vivid details as possible. You might want to give some examples.

    As the title suggests, think of the game in terms of Ping-Pong: each time the ball comes your way, aim as best as you can and give it your best swipe. There isn't a lot of time to think about where or how you want to hit the ball. The same goes for your storytelling turn. If you wait too long thinking about what you're going to add to the story, the game loses momentum and the other players might lose interest. The spontaneity and improvisation are a large part of what makes the game engaging.

other neat ideas

➤➤ Play Story Ping-Pong in the car.

➤➤ Play the game on an outdoor adventure, incorporating your surroundings into the story.

➤➤ Use a timer to put a limit on the story. This adds a bit of suspense to the game.

➤➤ Write down the story in order to preserve it or to use it as Story Starter on another day.

1, 2, 3 Scribble & Tell

This energetic activity is based on the game in which one player scribbles and another turns the random lines into something recognizable. In this version, the players interpret their own scribbles and tell stories about the pictures, too.

TIME
1 hour

AGES
4+

PLAYERS
3+

MATERIALS
➤ art markers
➤ crayons and/or colored pencils
➤ scrap paper

HOW TO DO IT

1. You'll need one leader and one or more players. Although the game works with only one player, it's more fun and interesting with more.

2. All players should be seated at a table with an art marker, a cup of crayons or colored pencils, and a short stack of blank scrap paper. The leader starts the game by saying, "One, two, three, scribble." When the players hear the word *scribble,* they begin drawing random scribbles. After a few seconds of scribbling, the leader says, "Stop," and the players immediately put down their pencils or crayons.

3. Players examine all the scribbles on their papers, thinking about what kind of imaginary creatures, places, faces, or scenes might be found within the random lines and curves.

4. Next, they use their art markers and colored pencils to add lines and color, so the scribbles begin to depict part of a story — a character or a place, for example. Encourage players to add lines and curves to their drawing as needed, but be sure the original scribble remains significant.

5. Once their drawings are complete, players take turns sharing them with the group. The drawings might be part of a larger group story.

other neat ideas

➤➤ Give players in 1, 2, 3 Scribble & Tell the same photocopied scribble, and ask them to turn it into some aspect of a story. Compare creations at the end.

➤➤ Players can write a short story based on their scribble creation.

➤➤ As a challenge, give the players a theme or topic for their creations.

Story Timeline

This detailed, illustrated, chronological timeline gives children practice with sequencing and paring down to the most elemental, important aspects of a story. After hearing a friend's story, children work together (or alone) to create a tailored but complete timeline of what happens.

TIME
1–2 hours

AGES
6+ (the older the child, the more complex and detailed the story and timeline will be)

PLAYERS
3+ (can be modified to be a 1-player activity)

MATERIALS
➤ painter's tape
➤ a long piece of rolled paper
➤ yardstick
➤ thick black marker
➤ pencils
➤ art markers
➤ colored pencils

Not only is this great practice for the story listeners but it's also extremely useful for the storyteller, as she hears others determine the important events in her tale. In essence, children are learning important outlining skills as they chronologically deconstruct a story.

HOW TO DO IT

1. Tape a long piece of rolled white paper onto a wall or the floor. If you are concerned about damaging your wall, use painter's tape, which is designed for easy removal. It's a good idea to double your paper to avoid any bleeding through. Use the yardstick and a marker to draw a line down the center of the length of the paper.

THIS TOWN HAS A SUNFLOWER FIELD!

2. Have one child read aloud (or tell) one of her previously created stories. For this activity to work well, the story should be thought out, with an interesting beginning, middle, and end. If the story is vague and incomplete, it will probably be very challenging for the listeners to create a timeline.

3. The listeners recall and discuss the story in its entirety, then decide on the most important aspects of the plot as they occurred chronologically. One member of the group should be keeping notes on a separate piece of paper. Once the group is in agreement about the list, the children begin creating the visual timeline. Each member (including the storyteller) takes a turn writing an event on the timeline and drawing a picture to go along with it. If the paper is long enough, a few children can be writing and drawing at the same time.

   In the end, as children read the timeline together, they will enjoy the eclectic visual interpretations of the story.

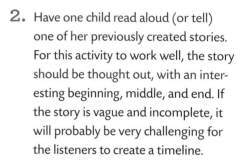

➤ **TEACHING TIPS**
Ask students to make their own individual timeline of a story or novel they just read in class or of a story they just wrote.

other neat ideas

>> Make the Story Timeline without words, then take turns retelling the story just by looking at the pictures.

>> Make a timeline of the story of your own life up until age 110.

Timing Is Everything

This unstructured storytelling group game asks children to throw their careful plans out the window and surrender to the moment. The purpose of this activity is to have storytellers relinquish control of their work and to practice a flexible, spontaneous kind of storytelling. It is the ultimate collaborative story; instead of being in charge of how much they add to the story, children rely on the buzz of a timer to tell them when to start and stop. This game is best played with at least four storytellers, along with one person, called the leader, who is in charge of the timer.

TIME
1 hour

AGES
5+

PLAYERS
5+

MATERIAL
➤ timer that buzzes, dings, or beeps (an online timer works)

HOW TO PLAY

1. The storytellers sit in a circle, with the leader off to the side. Children take turns telling a bit of a story, but the hitch is that they must begin their portion when the leader says

other neat ideas

>> Play Timing Is Everything at a birthday party.

>> For a challenge, the leader can give the group a topic or theme to stick to.

>> An adult can record the game and play it back for the group so they can hear and enjoy their newly created story.

go and end when the timer buzzes. Just before saying go and before a player tells a new part of the story, the leader sets the timer to a random amount of time, being sure to make it different for each player. (Some turns will be very short, like 20 seconds, and some will be long, like 2 minutes; for the sake of the momentum of the game, each turn shouldn't be longer than that.) The trick is for the players to try to ignore the possibility of the buzz or ding and tell an interesting, uninhibited story. It might feel difficult to end midsentence, but players should be encouraged to end promptly at the sound of the buzzer — that's what makes the game exciting.

2. The players take turns until the group feels that the story is finished. If time allows, new stories can be told and each child can have a chance to be the leader.

3. An adult can reflect with the children and discuss how it felt to have other people develop their ideas. Were there instances when other players continued with their ideas in a likeminded direction? Did the narrative go in a completely different and surprising direction? Discuss how both scenarios felt (funny, frustrating, exciting, interesting, and so on).

magical
mailbox

. . . there once was a magical mailbox that granted every wish you delivered to it . . .

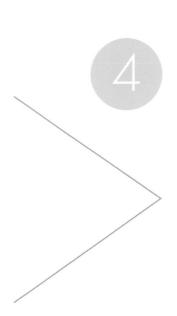

4 story play

all the brainstorming, story starting, and storytelling come to life

Fantasy is an exercise bicycle for the mind. It might not take you anywhere, but it tones up the muscles that can.

— TERRY PRATCHETT

The imaginative projects here are meant to inspire and support children as they act out their creative storytelling. They give children the chance to express their stories through drama and fantasy play.

As you read, keep in mind that there isn't one right way to make and play with these projects. How you use the ideas and projects depends on a particular child's inclinations. You can introduce and make a project with children, such as the Magic Flower Wand (page 118), and then set them off to play with it. Or if you overhear your child playing fairies in the backyard, *then* make the Magic Flower Wand. Just keep these projects in mind as you observe children playing and telling stories.

→ There (still) isn't one right way.

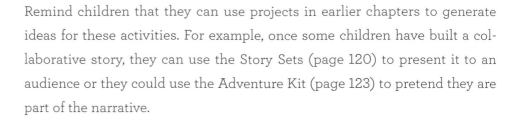

Remind children that they can use projects in earlier chapters to generate ideas for these activities. For example, once some children have built a collaborative story, they can use the Story Sets (page 120) to present it to an audience or they could use the Adventure Kit (page 123) to pretend they are part of the narrative.

In some situations, it will be helpful for you to model ways to incorporate these handcrafted playthings into children's play. Drop messages into the Magical Mailbox (page 115), cast spells with the Magic Flower Wand, or pretend to explore a cave in which Magic Pebbles (page 117) reside.

She came back the next day to find a secret message . . .

Magical Mailbox

This whimsical mailbox is designed to house magical notes from both real and imaginary friends. Hang it by the door to encourage an ongoing dialogue between your children and their pretend friends. You can become a part of your children's correspondence by dropping little notes and gifts into the mailbox. This game serves as a way for children to be reflective if they decide to ask their mystical friends for help or guidance.

TIME
To make: 2 hands-on hours

AGES
To make: 5+

To use: 3+

PLAYERS
1+

MATERIALS
- square tissue box
- 1 cereal- or cracker-box panel
- pencil
- ruler
- scissors
- craft knife
- masking tape
- white acrylic paint
- a brightly colored paint
- collage materials or a mini garland
- cardstock
- craft glue
- nail (or awl)
- 1" fastener
- twine
- picture hanging hook
- hammer

HOW TO MAKE

1. Set the tissue box topside down on the cereal-box panel. With a pencil, trace the shape of the square top. Measure with a ruler to add an extra ½" on one side to make it a rectangle, then round the corners to make the overhang curved. Cut along the lines. This will be the mailbox's lid.

2. To create the box itself, have an adult cut off the top of the tissue box with the craft knife. Put the lid on top of the open mailbox and secure on one side with masking tape: this will create a flexible hinge. The lid should have an inch of rounded overlap on the front of the box.

3. Paint the box, lid, and masking-tape hinge with white acrylic paint. Once fully dry, coat with the brightly colored paint, let the paint dry, then coat again. If you'd like to give the mailbox definition, paint the lid a different color or a few shades darker than the mailbox.

Trace the lid, adding extra for an overhang.

Cut the lid off a tissue box.

4. Use paint or glue on some collage materials or a mini garland to decorate the mailbox. Some possibilities: dried flowers, shells, felt circles, mini–paper pendants, and front door and windows.

5. To create a mailbox flag, cut a 5" × 1" rectangle out of cardstock. Next, decide what shape you would like for the flag: a star, acorn, flower, rabbit, or a typical flag shape. The possibilities are endless. Cut the shape out of the boxboard and glue it to the top of the skinny rectangle.

6. To attach the flag to the box, turn the mailbox so that the left side is facing you and place your finger on the bottom edge of the box. Finding the approximate center of the edge, measure 1½" up from the bottom and mark with a pencil. Poke a hole there with the nail or awl. Then, make another hole ½" up from the bottom of the flag. Match the two holes, place a fastener through, and secure inside the mailbox. The attached flag will now move up and down to show whether or not there's mail.

7. To create a hanger on the back, use the nail or awl to punch two parallel holes in the back of the box. Feed a 12" piece of twine through the holes and tie tight to create a loop that has some tension. Once the loop is secure, hang the box from a picture hanging hook hammered into the wall.

Magic Pebbles

Give a child a bucket of colorful Magic Pebbles and anything is possible! These simple, brightly hued stones are surprisingly stimulating props for telling stories about a magical land, a treasure hunt, fairies, a sea adventure, and superheroes, for example. Sprinkle them throughout your backyard, hide them in the living room, or simply give your children buckets of them. Chances are they'll begin to create stories around them by sorting, packing, hiding, selling, and gifting them.

HOW TO MAKE

1. Wash the stones in a bucket of water. Swish them around to wash away the dirt, then lay them on a dishtowel to dry.

2. When the pebbles are fully dry, paint them a variety of colors. (If you or your children want to keep colors bright and true, put out only a few stones and one color at a time. This way, you'll avoid having mostly brownish gray rocks.) Once they're coated with paint, set them on wax paper to dry, then repaint the undersides to ensure a full coat.

3. After they're fully dry from the second painting, give the multicolored magical stone collection to your children to play with.

TIME
To make: 1 hour

AGES
To make: 3+

To use: 3+

PLAYERS
1+

MATERIALS
> smooth pebbles of all shapes and sizes
> bucket of water
> dish towel
> paintbrushes
> craft paint
> wax paper

Magic Flower Wand

This woodland magic wand, made with flowers and leaves, casts enchanting spells. Children can incorporate it into any kind of magical play. It is durable and long lasting, making it perfect for both inside and outside play.

TIME
To make: 1 hour

AGES
To make: 5+
(with an adult)

To use: 3+

PLAYERS
1+

MATERIALS
- small handsaw
- ¼" wooden dowel
- wire clippers
- artificial flowers with stems and leaves
- green ribbon or raffia (for binding)
- decorative ribbon (for embellishing)
- craft glue

HOW TO MAKE

1. With the handsaw, an adult cuts the dowel to 16–18" long. Then, using the wire clippers, the adult snips two stems approximately 4" below the flowers. Be sure to leave some leaves and greenery for a natural, organic fairy-wand effect.

2. The child puts one stem on one side of the top of the dowel and, with the green ribbon, binds the stem to the dowel.

3. To ensure that the flower stays nice and tight, start at the top and bind the ribbon down the entire length of the stem (not the entire length of the dowel). Next, use a bit of craft glue on the ribbon and stem to set them for good. If a child finds the process of tying the ribbon difficult, she can use green florist's tape instead. The ribbon enables more of the leaves to poke through, whereas florist's tape will bind a bit more of the leaves to the dowel.

4. Once the glue has dried, tie some long pieces of decorative ribbon onto the top of the dowel. Use bunches of leaves as an anchor for the ribbon so it doesn't slip down the dowel.

Story Sets

This summer, as Hazel and I slid ourselves into small classroom chairs to watch Leah's creative-arts camp performance, I was immediately smitten with the handmade stage transformation. The "stage" was set with child-made, cartoonlike sets and props that were both fantastical and playful. The actors trekked through forests of cardboard trees, swam with a long cardboard whale, and held cardboard lanterns; these sets were just what they needed to make their play feel real. Story Sets will infuse magical realism into any living room, classroom, or outdoor production.

TIME
To make: 2 hands-on hours

AGES
To make: 5+ (with adult help)

To use: 3+

PLAYERS
1+

MATERIALS
- pencil
- large panels of cardboard box (at least 2')
- thick paintbrushes
- acrylic paint
- box cutter (to be used by an adult)
- scissors
- duct tape

HOW TO MAKE

1. Using the pencil, draw the shape of your prop onto a large cardboard-box panel.

2. Paint the inside of the shape with various colors.

3. When the paint is dry, an adult uses the box cutter to carefully (and safely) cut along the outside edge of the outline.

4. With the scissors, cut a separate rectangle of cardboard, bend it, and duct-tape it to the back to make a stand that keeps the Stage Set right.

HOW TO USE

Children can make their imaginary world come to life by arranging these on the floor of a room or outdoor space. Encourage children to interact with the Story Sets during their storytelling: sit under the pretend mushroom, carry the treasure box, feed soup to the baby bird (below), for example.

other neat ideas

>> Make Story Sets to decorate a child's room: try a giant rocket ship and a flag.

>> Make accessories such as the soup pot and spoon in the photo (above). Make a pirate flag, a wand, a computer, a guitar, cupcakes, or an ice-cream cone.

>> Play with scale and make a giant version of normally small things, such as the mushroom (right), or a large button, pair of scissors, carrot, jewel, envelope, or a bumblebee.

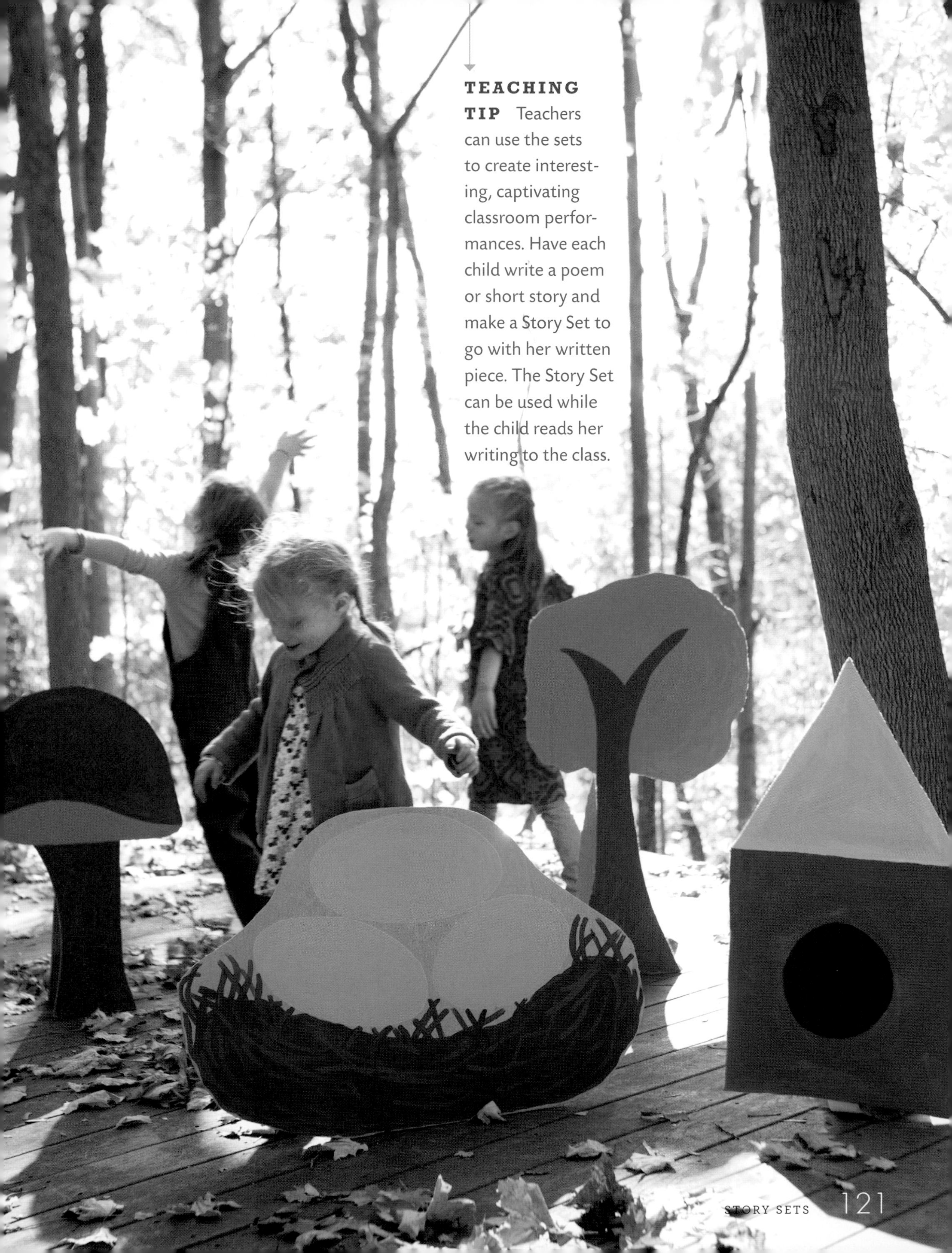

TEACHING TIP Teachers can use the sets to create interesting, captivating classroom performances. Have each child write a poem or short story and make a Story Set to go with her written piece. The Story Set can be used while the child reads her writing to the class.

AGES
To make: 5+
To play: 5+

PLAYERS
1+

TREASURE MAP TIME
To make: 1 hour

MATERIALS
- scissors
- newsprint
- ruler
- pencil
- waterproof black art marker
- colored markers
- watercolors
- colored pencils

Adventure Kit

With badges, treasure maps, binoculars, and an adventure book, your children will be lost for hours in their own epic journeys and quests.

Treasure Map

1. Trim a sheet of newsprint to an approximately 15" square. With the pencil, draw long and twisty paths with lots of details. Consider drawing geographical features, such as mountains, deserts, cities, bodies of water, and obstacles (a prickly forest or a cave with a monster, for example). At the end of one of the paths, draw something to denote a treasure.

2. Go over the pencil lines with markers or colored pencils, and write in the names of towns, rivers, mountain ranges, and roads. Use the watercolors to brighten the map.

3. When it's dry, fold your map into a small package to take along on an adventure. Make as many Treasure Maps as needed.

Adventure Kit

ADVENTURE BADGE

TIME
To make: 1 hour

MATERIALS

➤ pencil

➤ cereal-box panels

➤ scissors

➤ paintbrushes

➤ acrylic paint

➤ Q-tip

➤ glue

➤ glitter

➤ black art pen

➤ stencils (optional)

➤ alphabet stamps (optional)

➤ hot-glue gun (or extra-strong craft glue)

➤ large safety pin

Official Adventure Badges

1. Use the template (page 135) to trace a badge onto a cereal-box panel. Carefully cut out the badge, then paint it with a nice bright color. Let dry.

2. If you'd like, use a Q-tip to apply a thin layer of glue to the tips of the badge and sprinkle glitter on the wet glue. When the glitter is fully dry, use the black art pen, stencils, or stamps to write your child's imaginary name and title: perhaps Explorer, Spy, Guide, Snoop, Eagle Eye, or Top Sleuth.

3. Use the hot-glue gun to affix a safety pin to the back of the badge.

ADVENTURE BOOK

TIME
To make: 1 hour

MATERIALS

➤ blank Storybook

➤ alphabet stencil or stamps

➤ pencil

Adventure Book

See directions for the Storybook (page 72). Using alphabet stamps, write the title: *Adventure Book*. Children can record pictures and summaries of their adventures in it.

BINOCULARS
MATERIALS
TIME
To make: 1 hour

MATERIALS
- ➤ two toilet-paper tubes for each pair of binoculars
- ➤ paintbrushes
- ➤ acrylic paint
- ➤ yarn
- ➤ craft glue
- ➤ clothespins
- ➤ wax paper
- ➤ hole punch

Spy Binoculars

1. Coat both of the toilet-paper tubes with acrylic paint, then set aside to dry. While they are drying, trim a piece of yarn to 32" (adjust the length to fit comfortably over the child's head).

2. When the tubes are fully dry, coat the length of one tube with craft glue and firmly press the other tube onto the glued area. As you coat the tube, make an effort to apply glue only to the area where the other tube will soon be. Hold them together for a full minute, clamping on each end with clothespins, and set them on a piece of wax paper to dry.

3. Once dry, punch a hole at the top of the outside of each tube and tie the ends of the yarn to each side, making sure the knots are inside the tubes.

4. (Optional) To turn the binoculars into super-magical spy gear, place a circle of colored cellophane wrap (½" larger than the diameter of the tubes) at the end of each tube and secure with colorful rubber bands. These form the "lenses."

Use a tiny suitcase or satchel as your secret case, and you're ready to go!

Story Scenery

TIME
To make: **4+ hours**

AGES
To make: **5+ (an adult
helps with sewing)**

To use: **3+**

PLAYERS
1+

MATERIALS
- various patterned fab-
  rics, for the appliqués
- fabric pencil
- fabric scissors
- 48" × 39" piece of
  white (or natural)
  cotton material
- pins
- sewing machine
  (optional)
- needle and thread
- one 12" square
  wool felt
- fabric paint (optional)

Pin this oversized backdrop onto the wall or a wide doorframe, or attach to two trees for a quick way to transform your children's space into a magical scene. The appliqués on the backdrop create an enticing, transforming display. Make different scenes for as many story-play adventures as your children are interested in.

HOW TO MAKE

1. Determine what will be in your scene. For my camping scene, I chose to include a campfire, some tents, a clothesline, and a tree. (As a gauge, the tents are 18" and 23" tall.) Adjust the scene to the children's preferences.

2. Draw and cut out oversized details in various printed fabrics. Pin and stitch them onto the white backdrop. Do this until the scenery is exactly the way the children like it.

3. For easy hanging, cut the felt into three 3" squares. Place them in the top corners and top center of the fabric, pin in place, and use a zigzag stitch to attach them to the scenery. Use the scissors to cut a ½" slit in each square, which will be used to hang the scenery onto nails.

4. Hang on a wall or between two trees for imaginative fantasy play.

CRAFT TIPS

➤ Don't forget to add enticing details, such as doors, windows, and chimneys on the houses, and food on the plates.

➤ Use fabric paint to help make your scene instead of (or in addition to) the appliqué fabrics.

Simple Doorway Stage

Use 2 to 4 yards of plush velour and an adjustable curtain rod to make a stage out of any door frame. If you can find wide enough fabric for your doorway, cut 2 yards of fabric lengthwise to make the curtain panels. If you want more generous curtains, use 4 yards and cut into two 2-yard pieces. Make a 3-inch casing along the top of each panel to insert the curtain rod (or a rope hung with two nails). Add fancy gold embellishments and ties to give the curtain a grand presence. Take a bow.

story scene ideas

Use this technique to create a backdrop for your child's favorite kind of imaginary play:

>> a beach
>> a grassy hill
>> the moon
>> a farm
>> a birthday party
>> up in the air (with birds and airplanes)

materials

The supplies listed here are those I love and rely on. I use them often in my crafting, and they can be reused again and again for the activities in this book. Refer to the individual materials lists for each project, as there are some unique materials, such as plywood and magnetic primer paint, that are not listed below. You'll find that many of the projects can be made with materials you have on hand in your pantry, cabinets, yard, drawers, and recycling bin. Almost all of the materials and tools needed to complete the projects can be found at local art and craft supply shops. For those you can't find locally, check out the following list of online resources.

When I *do* shop for craft materials, I tend to buy quality tools and supplies. In my experience, well-made art supplies enable more flexibility and artistic expression. It's sometimes easier to make do with less expensive versions, and boy, they do have their merits in certain situations, but quality materials generally end up being more satisfying. And when children are satisfied with their artwork, they're more likely to want to create more.

If you are careful with your supplies, they will last for a nice stretch of time. For the sake of your wallet, I don't suggest replacing supplies in one fell swoop. Slowly infiltrate your supply shelves with high-quality items.

MARKERS, PENS, AND PENCILS

➤ Micron markers 0.2 and 0.3 in black
Black is critical, but experiment with various sizes and colors.

➤ Sharpies
These come in fine and super-fine tips.

➤ graphic pencils
Use for sharp, detailed drawing. Experiment with different hardness/softness grades.

➤ colored pencils
Quality pencils impart more satisfying richness of color than do the most basic versions.

PAINTS

➤ acrylic paints

➤ liquid watercolors

PAPERS

➤ origami papers

➤ watercolor paper

➤ newsprint

➤ sketchpads

➤ brightly colored cardstock

SEWING AND STITCHING SUPPLIES

➤ cotton embroidery thread

➤ embroidery needles

➤ hemp craft cord

➤ waxed linen cord

➤ fabric

➤ small embroidery scissors

➤ fabric scissors

STICKY STUFF

➤ decoupage medium Mod Podge

➤ glue stick
Look for one that is acid-free, archival, washable, and long lasting.

➤ all-purpose craft glue

➤ masking tape
These come in a variety of colors (see next page).

TOOLS

➤ sharp paper scissors (with adult supervision)

➤ craft knife (with extra blades and adult supervision)

➤ hole punch (both ⅛" and ¼")

➤ corner-rounding punch

➤ bone folder
This helps to make nice creases. You can also use the back of a spoon.

➤ non-smudge eraser

➤ paintbrushes (various sizes . . . a small one is handy)

➤ foam brushes

➤ ruler

EXTRAS

➤ wooden disks
These come in 1½" and ½" diameters (see next page).

➤ alphabet stamps

➤ pigment and dye ink pads

FAVORITE FOUND MATERIALS

➤ small rocks and stones

➤ cereal-box panels

➤ yogurt cups and plastic takeout food containers (for paint, water, and brushes)

➤ egg cartons (for sorting)

➤ catalogs, magazines, newspapers, very worn, dilapidated picture books (found at garage sales and thrift stores), old dictionaries, postcards, scrap paper (for collage)

➤ old shirts, skirts, dresses (for repurposed fabric)

➤ jars

➤ buttons

➤ old maps

➤ record album covers

➤ stacks of used printer paper from the recycling bin in offices and schools (for jotting down design notes and lists)

➤ brown paper grocery bags (for craft paper and table coverings)

➤ pinecones

➤ small shells

➤ bits of string and yarn

Online Shops

These sites sell specialty materials as well as those that are a bit more difficult to track down. Check out www.etsy.com for lots of interesting shops that sell beautiful, unique supplies.

ART AND CRAFT SUPPLIES

Dick Blick Art Materials
800-828-4548
www.dickblick.com

Nasco
800-558-9595
www.enasco.com

BOOK-BINDING SUPPLIES

For awls, twine, tape, and so on
Hollander's
734-741-7531
www.hollanders.com

Paper Source
888-727-3711
www.paper-source.com

COLORFUL PAPER MASKING TAPE

Happytape
www.happytape.bigcartel.com

FABRIC

A Child's Dream Come True
800-359-2906
www.achildsdream.com
100% wool felt

Fabricworm
fabricworm@gmail.com
www.fabricworm.com

Purl Soho
800-597-7875
www.purlsoho.com

Spoonflower, Inc.
919-886-7885
www.spoonflower.com

superbuzzy
805-643-4143
www.superbuzzy.com

OPEN SOURCE PHOTO SITES

flickr
www.flickr.com
Go to the Open Source Photography [OSP] group

Open Clip Art Library
www.openclipart.org

WOODEN DISKS, CUBES, AND DOWELS

American Woodcrafters Supply Co.
800-995-4032
www.americanwoodcrafterssupply.com

Cardinal Woods
800-407-5090
www.cardinalenterprises.com

Woodworks, Ltd.
817-581-5230
www.craftparts.com

STORAGE TIP

It's frustrating when I don't have the exact material I need when I need it, so I store my most frequently needed repurposed materials in milk crates in the garage (a basement, closet, or a bin underneath a bed would do just as well). For example, I always have a medium-sized box full of smooth stones and a milk crate full of cereal-box panels. The key is to maintain a fairly small collection, as a large collection has the potential to feel overwhelming. Keep just a few of each item, and then when you use one, replace it. This way you'll always have a nice supply without feeling swamped with materials.

templates

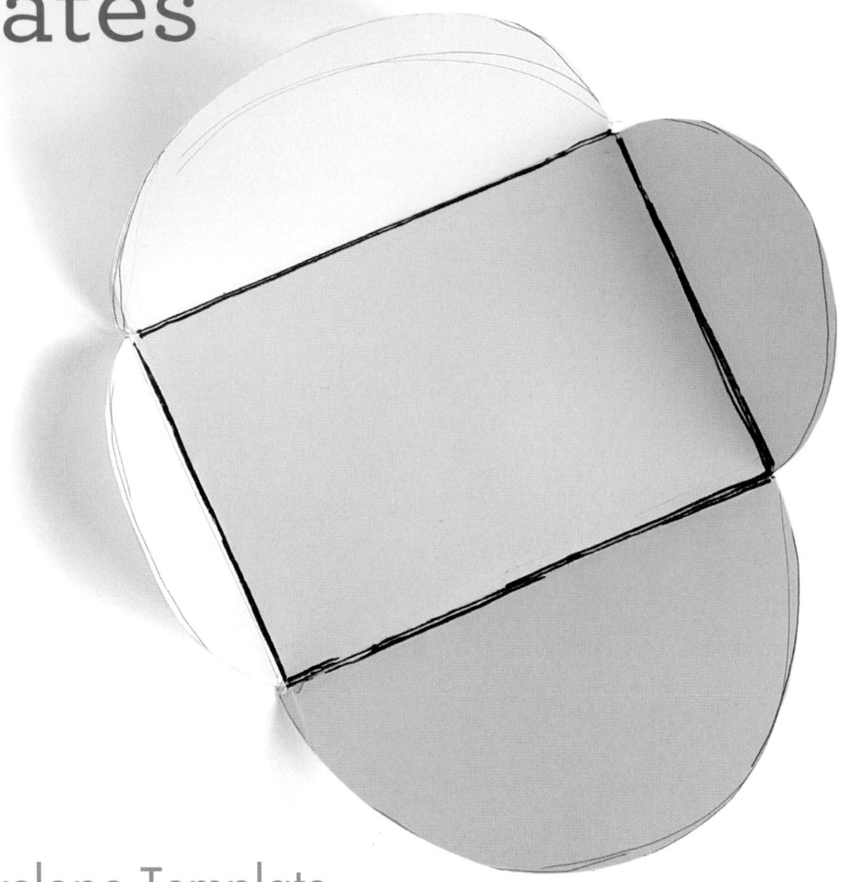

Envelope Template

This template is to make envelopes for storing game pieces and prompts. Use any kind of paper to create the envelopes, and tailor an envelope's size to what you intend to store in it. If you decide on a busily patterned paper, use plain labels on the front to clearly identify what's inside.

HOW TO MAKE

MATERIALS
- paper
- scissors
- bone folder
- glue stick

1. Carefully trace the template onto a piece of paper, then cut it out.

2. Fold the envelope firmly along the dotted lines. Use a bone folder to make sharp creases.

3. With a glue stick, glue the side panels together, being careful not to get any on the inside of the envelope. Glue the bottom flap onto the newly glued front panel.

4. Fold down the top flap but don't glue it.

5. When the envelope is dry, it's ready for you to group and store small pieces of paper.

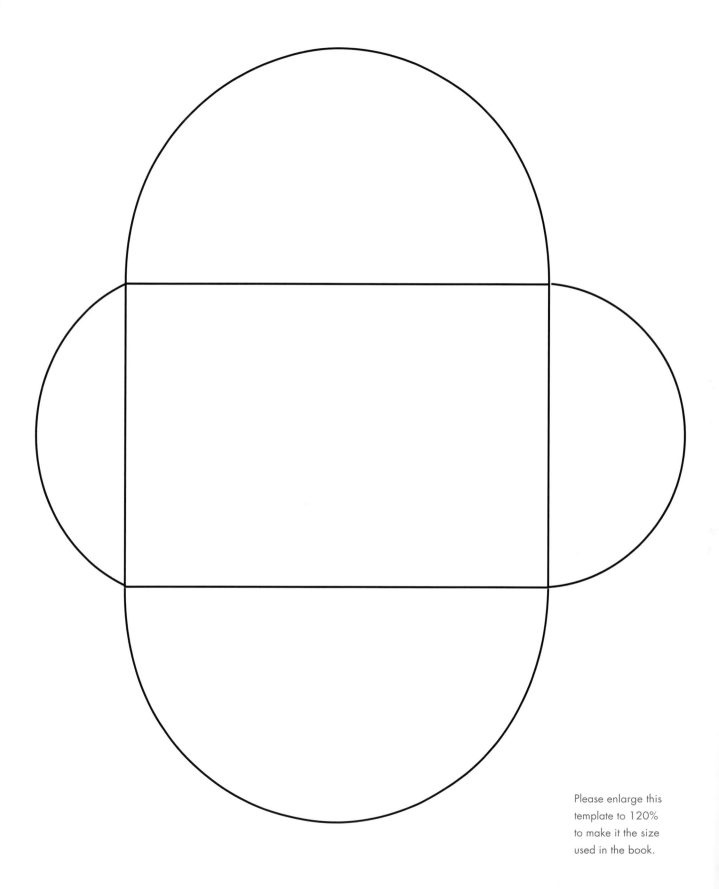

Please enlarge this template to 120% to make it the size used in the book.

Badge Template

This badge template is essential for the Adventure Kit on page 123, but it might come in handy for other role-playing games. To make the badge, see instructions on page 124.

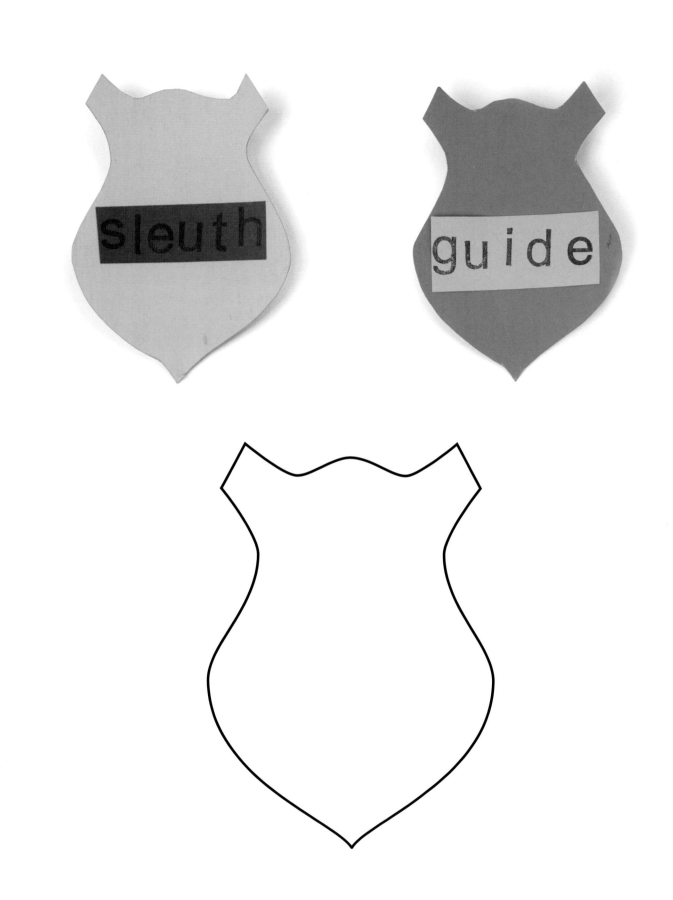

puppet theater

please see last pages in book

Puppets and Theaters

Use these charming storytelling theaters and the accompanying puppets to tell stories anywhere: in the car, snuggled on the couch, or just before bed. (Use the full directions in the Traveling Puppet Theater project on page 60 to make your own unique and fantastical versions.)

MATERIALS

- ➤ **wide tongue depressors (a.k.a. "craft sticks")**
- ➤ **craft glue**
- ➤ **glue stick**
- ➤ **wooden clothespins**
- ➤ **an empty cereal box (at least 10" tall)**
- ➤ **Mod Podge and foam brush**
- ➤ **ruler**
- ➤ **pencil**
- ➤ **craft knife**

HOW TO MAKE

1. Make color photocopies of the two theaters and puppets.

2. Carefully cut out each puppet. With a foam brush, coat the unprinted side of a cereal-box panel with a thin layer of Mod Podge. Place the images faceup on the panel and coat with another layer of Mod Podge, using your fingertips to smooth out any air bubbles or wrinkles. Allow to dry overnight.

3. Carefully trim the cereal-box panel edges from the puppet. Apply craft glue to the back of each image and attach it to the top of a craft stick. Lay all glued sticks on a piece of paper and clamp each with a clothespin. Allow them to dry.

4. To make theater stage, trim the edges of the backdrop and set aside. Cut the top and bottom off a cereal box and cut it open along one corner. It should be at least 16" × 10". With a glue stick, apply glue to the cereal box panel and mount the theater onto it. Once dry, trim the edges of the mounted theater.

5. To cut slits in the theater stage, using a ruler, draw two straight lines on the back of the theater stage, each about 3" long. Make one on the left part of stage and another on the right. Cut the slits with craft knife.

6. Slide the puppets through the slits and begin telling stories.

puppets

triceratops

brachiosaur

puppets

miss duckie

wolfie

mr. pup

miss mole

interior photography credits

© **Buff Strickland:** 2, 3, 6, 8, 10 bottom, 13, 18, 20 bottom, 23, 27, 31, 32 top, 33, 34, 37, 39 left, 41, 44, 45 top, 47, 50, 52, 54 bottom, 56, 57, 58 right, 59 lower right, 64, 66, 68, 72, 76, 79, 82, 84 bottom, 87, 91, 96, 97 top, 98, 102, 105, 107 left, 109, 110–111, 112 bottom, 114 bottom, 116 top, 117, 118–119, 120, 121, 122, 125 top, 126, 127 bottom, and 134

Carolyn Eckert: 15, 16, 106, and 127 top

Greg Nesbit Photography: 17, 24, 25, 30, 32 bottom, 35, 42, 43, 45 bottom, 46, 48, 49, 58 left (series), 59 except lower right, 60, 62, 63, 67 right, 74 bottom, 75, 77, 78 right, 80, 89, 93 top, 94, 95, 99, 100, 107 right, 116 bottom, 119 right, 124, 125 bottom, 135, and the puppet theater (left & right flaps)

John Polak Photography: 5, 22, 26, 28, 38, 39 right, 40, 61, 65, 67 left & center, 69, 70, 71, 73, 74 top, 78 left & center, 83, 88, 90, 93 bottom, 97 bottom, 101, 108, 111 bottom, 115, 123, and 132

Marcelino Vilaubi: 104 and the puppet theater (inside right spread)

© **Tara Gorman:** 1, 7, 10 top, 20 top, 54 top, 81, 84 top, 86, 112 top, 114 top, 128, 131, 140, 142, 144, and the puppet theater (front & back panels, inside left spread)

acknowledgments

My deep, heartfelt thanks to Deborah Balmuth, for believing in my work from the beginning. To Pam Thompson, Carolyn Eckert, and everyone at Storey Publishing, for their energy, care, and dedication. And to Buff Strickland and Tara Gorman for their inspired photography.

To my parents, who from the beginning never fretted about my little hands perpetually covered in marker. To my mother, for being my biggest supporter and for teaching me to trust in my own creative process. You are my constant reminder that what is now is what is most beautiful. To my father, for the quiet nights on our couch reading stories, for welling up at the sad parts, and for long mystery road trips where the people we met became characters in our family lore. And, of course, for baking warm loaves of crusty bread after long days of writing.

To my Papa Joe and my Nanny Ruth, for delighting in everything I did, in every new path I took. To my Kaufman uncles, for their love, and to Auntie Lynn, for always being one supportive phone call away.

To the entire Neuburger family, for their love.

To Tracy, for her sisterly love and steadfast encouragement. To Kelly Bridges and Ariana Inglese, for inspiring me. To Maddie DelVicario, for being a kind and encouraging first reader who gave the feedback I needed to forge ahead.

To Camille Owens, for being the most wonderful, creative babysitter two kids could ever have; without you, my book proposal could not have been written.

To my workshop students, whose insights and creations fill me with joy every week.

To the lovely blog readers at Red Bird Crafts: Thank you for visiting, commenting, and supporting my work. You inspire me in the brightest of ways.

To my kitty, Sophie, for keeping my lap warm as I wrote long into the dark winter nights.

And to my children, who are my greatest joys. Leah Rose, thank you for your passion, your empathy, and your deep, uninhibited creative spirit. Your love notes kept me going when my mind was tired. Hazel Ruth, thank you for your hearty, unending enthusiasm, your willingness to be part of it all, the stories you whisper into my ear, and for the way you love me with your big blue eyes.

And to Tom — the most wonderful husband and papa to our little ones. When you look into my eyes, it is with confidence, warmth, patience, and love. And with that, I can do anything.

index

A

Adventure Kit, 122–25
    Adventure Book, 124
    Official Adventure Badges, 124
    Spy Binoculars, 125
    Treasure Map, 123
alphabet stamps, 38, 42

B

Badges, Official Adventure, 124
Beginning, Middle, End, 38–39
Binoculars, Spy, 125
Blocks, Story, 34–35
book, making a
    Adventure Book, 124
    how to bind, 73–74
    Storybook, 72–76
Build a Story, 96–97

C

camera, 17
Cards, Memory, 63–65
Chain, Story-Disk, 94–95
characters, developing, 13, 36–37, 51
City, Story, 77–79
collage, 24, 58–59, 63–65, 74
conflict and resolution, 36–37, 53
craft tools, 130
Create the Past, 104–5
Cut and Tell, 28–29

D

Dice, Story, 32–33
Disks, Story
    paper, 94–95
    wooden, 20, 23–27
doorway stage, 127

F

Fill In the Blanks, 92–93
Flower Wand, Magic, 118–19
found materials, 15, 57, 120

G

glues and adhesives, 130
Grab Bag, Story, 40–42
group storytelling, 47, 105
    Build a Story, 96–97
    Magnetic Story Board, 48–49
    Reference Desk, The, 102–3
    Story Grab Bag, 40–421
    Story Ping-Pong, 106
    Story Pool, 30–31
    These Are the Stories in My
        Neighborhood, 43–46
    Timing Is Everything, 110–11

I

inspiration, 14–16

J

Jar, Storytelling, 54, 68–71
journals, writing in, 17, 49

K

Kit, Adventure, 122–25
Kit, Storytelling, 83

L

library game, 102–3

M

Magic Flower Wand, 118–19
Magic Pebbles, 117
Magical Mailbox, 112, 114–16
Magnetic Story Board, 48–49
maps
    Story Map, 80–81
    Treasure Map, 123
Mat, Story, 66–67
materials, 128–31
memory book, 75
Memory Cards, 63–65
Mod Podge tips, 25

N

nature inspiration, 15–16
neighborhood stories
    Story City, 77–79
    Story Map, 80–81
    These Are the Stories in My
        Neighborhood, 43–47

O

objects in stories, 52
1, 2, 3 Scribble & Tell, 107
online shops, 131

P

papers, 130
parts of a story, 36–37
    characters, 36–37, 51
    conflict and resolution, 36–37, 53
    descriptive adjectives, 51
    events, 52
    objects, 52
    plot, 36–37
    setting, 36–37, 51
    theme, 36–37
    time, choosing a, 52
Pebbles, Magic, 117
photographs
    Cut and Tell, 28–29
    Picture Tales, 89
    Story Blocks, 34–35
Picture Tales, 89
plot, basic elements of, 36–37
    Beginning, Middle, End, 38–39
poems, writing, 71, 98–99, 121
portable projects, 56
problem-solving, 13, 53
Puppet Theater, Traveling, 60–62, 136–39

R

Reference Desk, The, 102–3

S

setting of a story, 36–37, 51
sewing
    Story Mat, 66–67
    Story Scenery, 126–27
    Storytelling Jar, 69–71
    supplies, 130
Soundtrack, Story, 82
stage, simple doorway, 127
stamping, 24–27, 32–33, 38, 42, 44–46
stones
    collecting, 57

stones (*continued*)
    Magic Pebbles, 117
    Story Stones, 57–59, 68, 71
storage tips, 131
Story Blocks, 34–35
Story City, 77–79
Story Dice, 32–33
Story Disks, 20, 23–27
Story Grab Bag, 40–42
Story Map, 80–81
Story Mat, 66–67
Story Ping-Pong, 106
Story Pool, 30–31
Story Scenery, 126–27
Story Sets, 120–21
Story Soundtrack, 82
Story Sparks, 50–51
Story Stones, 57–59, 68, 71
Story Tickets, 30–31
Story Timeline, 108–9
Story-Disk Chain, 94–95
Storybook, 72–76
Storytelling Jar, 54, 68–71
Storytelling Kit, 83
Storytelling Walk, 87–88

. . . and they lived happily ever after.

T

teaching tips, 18–19
templates
    badge, 134–45
    envelope, 132–33
    puppets, 136–39
theater
    simple doorway stage, 127
    Story Scenery, 126–27
    Story Sets, 120–21
    Traveling Puppet Theater, 60–62
theme, choosing a, 36–37, 41, 59
These Are the Stories in My Neighborhood,
    43–47
time, choosing a, 52
Timeline, Story, 108–9
Timing Is Everything, 110–11
tools for crafts, 130
Traveling Puppet Theater, 60–62, 136–39
treasure map, 80–81, 123
Truth or Tale?, 90–91

V

vocabulary, building, 24, 58
    Beginning, Middle, End, 38–39
    Fill In the Blanks, 92–93
    Reference Desk, The, 102–3
    Word Tags, 98–99

W

Walk, Storytelling, 87–88
Word Lists, 100–101
Word Tags, 98–99
writing
    creative writing exercise, 92–93
    implements, 130
    poems, 71, 98–99, 121
    short stories, 72–76, 104–5, 107, 121
    storybook, 76

puppet theater backgrounds

ahab's fish & chips